Judicial Activity Concerning Enemy Combatant Detainees: Major Court Rulings

Jennifer K. Elsea
Legislative Attorney

Michael John Garcia
Legislative Attorney

April 6, 2012

Congressional Research Service
7-5700
www.crs.gov
R41156

CRS Report for Congress
Prepared for Members and Committees of Congress

Summary

As part of the conflict with Al Qaeda and the Taliban, the United States has captured and detained numerous persons believed to have been part of or associated with enemy forces. Over the years, federal courts have considered a multitude of petitions by or on behalf of suspected belligerents challenging aspects of U.S. detention policy. Although the Supreme Court has issued definitive rulings concerning several legal issues raised in the conflict with Al Qaeda and the Taliban, many others remain unresolved, with some the subject of ongoing litigation.

This report discusses major judicial opinions concerning suspected enemy belligerents detained in the conflict with Al Qaeda and the Taliban. The report addresses all Supreme Court decisions concerning enemy combatants. It also discusses notable circuit court opinions addressing issues of ongoing relevance. In particular, it summarizes notable decisions which have (1) addressed whether the Executive may lawfully detain only persons who are "part of" Al Qaeda, the Taliban, and affiliated groups, or also those who provide support to such entities in their hostilities against the United States and its allies; (2) adopted a functional approach for assessing whether a person is "part of" Al Qaeda; (3) decided that a preponderance of evidence standard is appropriate for detainee habeas cases, but suggested that a lower standard might be constitutionally permissible, and instructed courts to assess the cumulative weight of evidence rather than each piece of evidence in isolation; (4) determined that Guantanamo detainees have a limited right to challenge their proposed transfer to foreign custody, but denied courts the authority to order detainees released into the United States; and (5) held that the constitutional writ of habeas does not presently extend to noncitizen detainees held at U.S.-operated facilities in Afghanistan. Finally, the report discusses a few criminal cases involving persons who were either involved in the 9/11 attacks (Zacarias Moussaoui) or were captured abroad by U.S. forces or allies during operations against Al Qaeda, the Taliban, and associated entities (John Walker Lindh and Ahmed Ghailani).

For over a decade, the primary legal authority governing the detention of enemy belligerents in the conflict with Al Qaeda was the 2001 Authorization for Use of Military Force ("AUMF," P.L. 107-40. In December 2011, Congress passed the National Defense Authorization Act for FY2012 ("2012 NDAA," P.L. 112-81), which contains a provision that is largely intended to codify the current understanding of the detention authority conferred by the AUMF, as has been interpreted and applied by the Executive and the D.C. Circuit. The full implications of the 2012 NDAA upon wartime detention jurisprudence remain to be seen. In any event, the act does not address many of the legal issues involving wartime detention that have not been squarely resolved by the Supreme Court. Among other things, these unresolved issues include the precise scope of the Executive's wartime detention authority, including the circumstances in which U.S. citizens may be detained; the degree to which noncitizens held abroad are entitled to protections under the Constitution; the authority of federal habeas courts to compel the release into the United States of detainees determined to be unlawfully held; and the ability of detainees to receive advance notice and to challenge their proposed transfer to foreign custody.

Several rulings addressed in this report are discussed in greater detail in other CRS products, including CRS Report RL33180, *Enemy Combatant Detainees: Habeas Corpus Challenges in Federal Court*, by Jennifer K. Elsea and Michael John Garcia; CRS Report RL34536, *Boumediene v. Bush: Guantanamo Detainees' Right to Habeas Corpus*, by Michael John Garcia; CRS Report RS21884, *The Supreme Court 2003 Term: Summary and Analysis of Opinions Related to Detainees in the War on Terrorism*, by Jennifer K. Elsea; and CRS Report R42337, *Detention of U.S. Persons as Enemy Belligerents*, by Jennifer K. Elsea.

Contents

Supreme Court Decisions 2
   Hamdi v. Rumsfeld, 542 U.S. 507 (2004) 2
   Rumsfeld v. Padilla, 542 U.S. 426 (2004) 3
   Rasul v. Bush, 542 U.S. 466 (2004) 3
   Hamdan v. Rumsfeld, 548 U.S. 557 (2006) 3
   Boumediene v. Bush, 553 U.S. 723 (2008) 4
   Gates v. Bismullah, 554 U.S. 913 (2008) 5
   al-Marri v. Spagone, 555 U.S. 1220 (2009) 5
   Kiyemba v. Obama, 130 S.Ct. 1235 (2010) 6
   Kiyemba v. Obama, 131 S. Ct. 1631 (2011) 6
Rulings by the D.C. Circuit Court of Appeals 6
   Scope of Executive's Detention Authority and Related Evidentiary Burdens 8
      Al-Bihani v. Obama, 590 F.3d 866, *en banc rehearing denied*,
         619 F.3d 1 (D.C. Cir. 2010), *cert. denied*, 131 S. Ct. 1814 (2011) 8
      Al-Adahi v. Obama, 613 F.3d 1102 (D.C. Cir. 2010), *cert. denied*,
         131 S. Ct. 1001 (2011) 10
      Awad v. Obama, 608 F.3d 1 (D.C. Cir. 2010), *cert. denied*, 131 S. Ct. 1814 (2011) 12
      Al Odah v. United States, 611 F.3d 8 (D.C. Cir. 2010), *cert. denied*, 131 S. Ct.
         1812 (2011) 13
      Bensayah v. Obama, 610 F.3d 718 (D.C. Cir. 2010) 14
      Salahi v. Obama, 625 F.3d 745 (D.C. Cir. 2010) 14
      Uthman v. Obama, 637 F.3d 400 (D.C. Cir. 2011) 16
      Al-Madhwani v. Obama, 642 F.3d 1071 (D.C. Cir. 2011) 17
      Almerfedi v. Obama, 654 F.3d 1 (D.C. Cir. 2011) 17
      Al Alwi v. Obama, 653 F.3d 11 (D.C. Cir. 2011) 19
      Latif v. Obama, 666 F.3d 746 (D.C. Cir. 2011) 20
   Transfer and Release of Detainees 22
      Kiyemba v. Obama, 555 F.3d 1022 (D.C. Cir. 2009) ("*Kiyemba I*"), *vacated*,
         130 S. Ct. 1235 (2010), *reinstated as amended*, 605 F.3d 1046 (D.C. Cir. 2010)
         ("*Kiyemba III*"), *cert. denied*, 131 S. Ct. 1631 (2011) 22
      Kiyemba v. Obama, 561 F.3d 509 (D.C. Cir. 2009) ("*Kiyemba II*"), *cert. denied*,
         130 S.Ct. 1880 (2010) 23
      Gul v. Obama, 652 F.3d 12 (D.C. Circ. 2011) 23
   Other Notable Rulings 24
      Parhat v. Gates, 532 F.3d 834 (D.C. Cir. 2008) 24
      Bismullah v. Gates, 551 F.3d 1068 (D.C. Cir. 2009) 25
      Rasul v. Myers, 563 F.3d 527 (D.C. Cir. 2009) (*per curiam*), *cert. denied*,
         130 S.Ct. 1013 (2009) 26
      Maqaleh v. Gates, 605 F.3d 84 (D.C. Cir. 2010) 27
      Al-Zahrani v. Rodriguez, 669 F.3d 315 (D.C. Cir. 2012) 28
Rulings by the Fourth Circuit Court of Appeals 28
   Padilla v. Hanft, 423 F.3d 386 (4th Cir. 2005) 28
   al-Marri v. Pucciarelli, 534 F.3d 213 (4th Cir. 2008) (*per curiam*) 30
   Lebron v. Rumsfeld, 670 F.3d 540 (4th Cir. 2012) 30
Criminal Cases 31
   Moussaoui Litigation 32

United States v. Lindh, 227 F. Supp. 2d 565 (E.D. Va. 2004) 34
United States v. Ghailani, No. S10 98 Crim. 1023 (S.D.N.Y.) 35
Conclusion 39

Contacts

Author Contact Information 40

As part of the conflict with the Taliban and Al Qaeda, the United States has captured and detained numerous persons believed to have been part of or associated with enemy forces. Over the years, federal courts have considered a multitude of petitions by or on behalf of suspected belligerents challenging aspects of U.S. detention policy. The Supreme Court has issued definitive rulings concerning several legal issues raised in the conflict with Al Qaeda and the Taliban, including executive authority under the 2001 Authorization for Use of Military Force ("AUMF," P.L. 107-40) to detain properly designated enemy belligerents captured on the Afghan battlefield; the application of at least some provisions of the 1949 Geneva Conventions to the conflict with Al Qaeda; and the ability of detainees held in the United States or at the U.S. Naval Station in Guantanamo Bay, Cuba, to challenge the legality of their detention in habeas corpus proceedings.

In December 2011, Congress passed the National Defense Authorization Act for FY2012 ("2012 NDAA," P.L. 112-81), which contains a provision largely intended to codify the present understanding of the detention authority conferred by the AUMF, as interpreted and applied by the Executive and the D.C. Circuit.[1] The full implications of the 2012 NDAA upon judicial activity concerning wartime detention remains to be seen. In any event, the act does not address many of the legal issues involving wartime detention which, while occasioning significant political debate, have not been squarely resolved by the Supreme Court. These issues include the full scope of the Executive's detention authority, including the circumstances in which U.S. citizens may be detained as enemy belligerents; the degree to which noncitizens held at Guantanamo and other locations outside the United States are entitled to protections under the Constitution; the authority of federal habeas courts to compel the release of detainees determined to be unlawfully held into the United States if the Executive cannot effectuate their release to another country; and the ability of detainees to receive advance notice and challenge their proposed transfer to a foreign country. Additionally, the Supreme Court may be called upon to determine the nature of procedural rules to be applied in habeas cases and the proper standard of evidence to be applied. To the extent that these rules are found to differ from the Federal Rules of Civil Procedure and other court rules, it may be necessary to determine whether the same procedural rules apply to both U.S. citizens and foreign nationals who may be detained under the AUMF authority.

This report briefly summarizes major judicial opinions concerning suspected enemy belligerents[2] detained in the conflict with Al Qaeda and the Taliban. It discusses all Supreme Court decisions concerning enemy combatants. It also addresses notable circuit court opinions addressing issues of ongoing relevance to U.S. detention policy. The report also discusses a few notable decisions by federal district courts, including criminal cases involving persons who were either involved in

---

[1] For further discussion of the detention provisions in the 2012 NDAA, see CRS Report R42143, *The National Defense Authorization Act for FY2012: Detainee Matters*, by Jennifer K. Elsea and Michael John Garcia. For an analysis of their application to U.S. persons, see CRS Report R42337, *Detention of U.S. Persons as Enemy Belligerents*, by Jennifer K. Elsea.

[2] The Obama Administration has discontinued the use of the term "enemy combatant" to describe persons detained pursuant to the law of war or the Authorization for Use of Military Force ("AUMF"). *See* Department of Justice (DOJ), "Department of Justice Withdraws 'Enemy Combatant' Definition for Guantanamo Detainees," press release, March 13, 2009, http://www.usdoj.gov/opa/pr/2009/March/09-ag-232.html (hereinafter "DOJ Press Release"); *In re Guantanamo Bay Detainee Litigation*, Respondents' Memorandum Regarding the Government's Detention Authority Relative to Detainees Held At Guantanamo Bay, No. 08-0442, filed March 13, 2009 (D.D.C.) (hereinafter "Detention Authority Memorandum"). We use the terms "enemy combatant" or "enemy belligerent" broadly to describe persons who might be subject to detention or prosecution in connection with the conflict authorized by the AUMF as interpreted by the executive branch.

the 9/11 attacks or were captured abroad by U.S. forces or allies during operations against Al Qaeda and the Taliban.

Many of the rulings discussed in this report are discussed in greater detail in other CRS products, including CRS Report RL33180, *Enemy Combatant Detainees: Habeas Corpus Challenges in Federal Court*, by Jennifer K. Elsea and Michael John Garcia; CRS Report RL34536, *Boumediene v. Bush: Guantanamo Detainees' Right to Habeas Corpus*, by Michael John Garcia; CRS Report RS21884, *The Supreme Court 2003 Term: Summary and Analysis of Opinions Related to Detainees in the War on Terrorism*, by Jennifer K. Elsea; and CRS Report R42337, *Detention of U.S. Persons as Enemy Belligerents*, by Jennifer K. Elsea.

Supreme Court Decisions

Since 2004, the Supreme Court has made several rulings concerning enemy combatants. These have addressed, *inter alia*, the Executive's authority to detain enemy belligerents under the 2001 AUMF; the legality of military commissions established by presidential order to try suspected belligerents for violations of the law of war; and detainees' access to federal courts.

Hamdi v. Rumsfeld, 542 U.S. 507 (2004)[3]

The *Hamdi* case addressed the President's authority to detain "enemy combatants" as part of the conflict authorized by the AUMF, and whether a detained individual could seek independent review of the legality of his detention. Four separate opinions were written, with none receiving support of a majority of the justices. However, a majority of the Court recognized that, as a necessary incident to the 2001 AUMF, the President is authorized to detain persons captured while fighting U.S. forces in Afghanistan (including U.S. citizens), and potentially hold such persons for the duration of the conflict to prevent their return to hostilities.[4] A divided Court found that persons deemed "enemy combatants" have the right to challenge the legality of their detention before a judge or other "neutral decision-maker," with a majority of the Justices clearly recognizing the existence of such a right in the case of a detained U.S. citizen.[5]

In a plurality opinion joined by three other Justices, Justice O'Connor wrote that a citizen detained as an enemy combatant must receive notice of the factual basis for his classification and a fair opportunity to rebut the government's factual assertions before a neutral decision-maker, and has a right to counsel in connection with such a hearing. The plurality suggested, however, that the exigencies of the circumstances of a detainee's capture may allow for a tailoring of enemy combatant proceedings "to alleviate their uncommon potential to burden the Executive at

---

[3] For further discussion of *Hamdi*, see CRS Report RS21884, *The Supreme Court 2003 Term: Summary and Analysis of Opinions Related to Detainees in the War on Terrorism*, by Jennifer K. Elsea; CRS Report R42337, *Detention of U.S. Persons as Enemy Belligerents*, by Jennifer K. Elsea.

[4] Hamdi v. Rumsfeld, 542 U.S. 507, 518 (2004) (O'Connor, J., plurality opinion); *id.* at 588-589 (Thomas, J., dissenting).

[5] *Id.* at 518, 533 (O'Connor, J., plurality opinion, joined by Breyer, J., Kennedy, J., and Rehnquist, C.J.); 553 (Souter, J., concurring in part and dissenting in part, joined by Ginsburg, J.). Justices Scalia and Stevens supported a more limited view concerning the Executive's authority to detain U.S. citizens, believing that detention without criminal charge was only permissible if Congress suspended the writ of habeas corpus. *Id.* at 554 (Scalia, J., dissenting, joined by Stevens, J.).

a time of ongoing military conflict," possibly allowing hearsay evidence and "a presumption in favor of the Government's evidence," as long as a fair opportunity to rebut such evidence is provided.[6]

Rumsfeld v. Padilla, 542 U.S. 426 (2004)[7]

The *Padilla* case, decided on the same day as *Hamdi*, concerned a habeas challenge by Jose Padilla, a U.S. citizen who was designated as an "enemy combatant" and militarily detained in the United States for his alleged involvement in an Al Qaeda plot to detonate a "dirty bomb." Unlike the petitioner in *Hamdi*, who was captured in the Afghan zone of combat, Padilla was captured on U.S. soil. In a 5-4 ruling, the Court remanded the case without deciding the merits on the ground that Padilla's habeas petition had not been filed in the proper venue. In doing so, the majority did not reach the merits of Padilla's claim that any authority the President might have under the AUMF to detain "enemy combatants" did not extend to persons captured on American soil and away from the Afghan battlefield. Four Justices would have found jurisdiction based on the "exceptional circumstances" of the case and affirmed the holding below that detention is prohibited under the Non-Detention Act, 18 U.S.C. §4001(a) (prohibiting the detention of U.S. citizens unless authorized by an act of Congress). Padilla filed a new petition in the Fourth Circuit, and the appellate court considered the legality of his detention in *Padilla v. Hanft*, discussed *infra*.

Rasul v. Bush, 542 U.S. 466 (2004)[8]

In *Rasul v. Bush*, the Court held in a 6-3 ruling that the federal habeas corpus statute, 28 U.S.C. §2241, provided federal courts with jurisdiction to consider habeas corpus petitions by or on behalf of persons detained at the U.S. Naval Station in Guantanamo Bay, Cuba. Having found that Guantanamo detainees were entitled by statute to seek habeas review of their detention, the Court did not reach the issue of whether the constitutional writ of habeas also extended to noncitizens held at Guantanamo. The Court also did not address whether a less rigorous burden of proof or relaxed evidentiary procedures would be appropriate in comparison to ordinary habeas cases. Congress subsequently attempted to limit the reach of the federal habeas statute to Guantanamo detainees through the enactment of the Detainee Treatment Act of 2005 (DTA)[9] and the Military Commissions Act of 2006 (MCA).[10]

Hamdan v. Rumsfeld, 548 U.S. 557 (2006)[11]

In *Hamdan v. Rumsfeld*, the Supreme Court reviewed the validity of military tribunals established pursuant to presidential order to try suspected terrorists for violations of the law of war. The

---

[6] *Id.* at 533-534 (O'Connor, J., plurality opinion).

[7] For further discussion of the *Padilla* decision, see CRS Report RS21884, *supra* footnote 3; CRS Report R42337, *supra* footnote 1.

[8] For a more detailed summary of the *Rasul* opinion, see CRS Report RS21884, *supra* footnote 3.

[9] P.L. 109-148, Title X; P.L. 109-163, Title XIV.

[10] P.L. 109-366.

[11] For further discussion of the *Hamdan* opinion, see CRS Report RS22466, *Hamdan v. Rumsfeld: Military Commissions in the "Global War on Terrorism,"* by Jennifer K. Elsea.

petitioner Hamdan was charged with conspiracy to commit a violation of the law of war. Prior to reaching the merits of the case, the *Hamdan* Court first had to determine whether the DTA stripped it of jurisdiction to review habeas corpus challenges by or on behalf of Guantanamo detainees whose petitions had already been filed prior to enactment of the DTA. In a 5-3 opinion, the Court held that the DTA did not apply to such petitions. Turning to the merits of the case, the majority held that the convened tribunals did not comply with the Uniform Code of Military Justice (UCMJ) or the law of war, as incorporated in the UCMJ and embodied in the 1949 Geneva Conventions, which the Court held applicable to the armed conflict with Al Qaeda. The Court concluded that, at a minimum, Common Article 3 of the Geneva Conventions applies to persons captured in the conflict with Al Qaeda, according to them a minimum baseline of protections, including protection from the "passing of sentences and the carrying out of executions without previous judgment pronounced by a regularly constituted court, affording all the judicial guarantees which are recognized as indispensable by civilized peoples." The Court held that military commissions were not "regularly constituted" because they deviated too far from the rules that apply to courts-martial, without a satisfactory explanation of the need for departing from such rules. In particular, the Court noted that the commission rules allowing the exclusion of the defendant from attending portions of his trial or hearing some of the evidence against him deviated substantially from court-martial procedures.

A four-justice plurality of the Court also recognized that for an act to be triable under the common law of war, the precedent for it being treated as an offense must be "plain and unambiguous."[12] After examining the history of military commission practice in the United States and internationally, the plurality further concluded that conspiracy to violate the law of war was not in itself a crime under the common law of war or the UCMJ.

Boumediene v. Bush, 553 U.S. 723 (2008)[13]

In the aftermath of the *Hamdan* decision, Congress enacted the MCA, which, *inter alia*, expressly eliminated court jurisdiction over all pending and future causes of action other than via the limited review permitted under the DTA. In the 2008 case of *Boumediene v. Bush*, the Court ruled in a 5-4 opinion that the constitutional privilege of habeas extends to Guantanamo detainees. In doing so, the Court stated that the Constitution's extraterritorial application turns on "objective factors and practical concerns."[14] The Court deemed at least three factors to be relevant in assessing the extraterritorial scope of the constitutional writ of habeas: (1) the citizenship and status of the detainee and the adequacy of the status determination process; (2) the nature of the site where the person is seized and detained; and (3) practical obstacles inherent in resolving the prisoner's entitlement to the writ.

The Court also found that MCA §7, which limited judicial review of executive determinations of the *Boumediene* petitioners' enemy combatant status to that authorized by the DTA, did not provide an adequate habeas substitute and therefore acted as an unconstitutional suspension of the writ of habeas corpus. The majority listed a number of potential constitutional infirmities in the DTA review process, including the absence of provisions (1) empowering a reviewing court to

---

[12] Hamdan v. Rumsfeld, 548 U.S. 557, 602 (2006) (Stevens, J., plurality opinion, joined by Souter, J., Ginsburg, J., and Breyer, J.).

[13] A more extensive discussion of *Boumediene* is found in CRS Report RL34536, *Boumediene v. Bush: Guantanamo Detainees' Right to Habeas Corpus*, by Michael John Garcia.

[14] Boumediene v. Bush, 553 U.S. 723, 764 (2008).

order the release of a detainee found to be unlawfully held; (2) permitting petitioners to challenge the President's authority to detain them indefinitely; (3) enabling a presiding court to review or correct administrative findings of fact which formed the legal basis for an individual's detention; and (4) permitting the detainee to present exculpatory evidence discovered after the conclusion of administrative proceedings.

Although the *Boumediene* Court held that the constitutional writ of habeas extends to noncitizens held at Guantanamo, it did not opine as to the scope of habeas review available to detainees, the remedy available for those persons found to be unlawfully held by the United States, or the extent to which other constitutional provisions extend to noncitizens held at Guantanamo and elsewhere.

Gates v. Bismullah, 554 U.S. 913 (2008)

Prior to the Supreme Court's decision in *Boumediene*, the D.C. Circuit Court of Appeals considered a number of challenges brought under the DTA in which detainees contested determinations by Combatant Status Review Tribunals (CSRTs) that they were properly detained as enemy combatants. In 2008, the government petitioned the Supreme Court to review two rulings by the D.C. Circuit regarding the scope of judicial review of CSRT determinations.[15] The Supreme Court granted certiorari and vacated the appellate court's decisions, remanding for reconsideration in light of the Supreme Court's decision in *Boumediene*. Upon remand, the D.C. Circuit reinstated without explanation its decisions, presumably because it did not find the *Boumediene* ruling to conflict with its decisions in these cases.

al-Marri v. Spagone, 555 U.S. 1220 (2009)

In December 2008, the Supreme Court granted certiorari to review an *en banc* ruling by the Fourth Circuit Court of Appeals regarding petitioner al-Marri, an alien lawfully admitted into the United States on a student visa who had been arrested by civilian law enforcement and thereafter transferred to military custody for detention as an enemy combatant. At the time, the Court's decision to review the Fourth Circuit's ruling was thought to have potentially set the stage for a definitive pronouncement regarding the President's authority to militarily detain terrorist suspects apprehended away from the Afghan battlefield. However, before the Court could consider the merits of the case, the government requested that the Court authorize al-Marri's release from military custody and transfer to civilian authorities to face criminal charges. The Court granted the government's request, vacated the appellate court's earlier judgment, and transferred the case back to the lower court with orders to dismiss it as moot. The appellate court's ruling is discussed in more detail below.

---

[15] The D.C. Circuit in July 2007 issued an order rejecting the government's motion to limit the scope of the court's review to the official record of the CSRT hearings. Bismullah v. Gates, 501 F.3d 178 (*Bismullah I*). The circuit court decided that in order to determine whether a preponderance of evidence supported the CSRT determinations, it must have access to all the information a CSRT is "authorized to obtain and consider, pursuant to the procedures specified by the Secretary of Defense." The court thereafter denied the government's request for rehearing, explaining its view that its previous order would not require a search for information that was not "reasonably available." Bismullah v. Gates, 503 F.3d 137(D.C. Cir. 2007) (*Bismullah II*).

Kiyemba v. Obama, 130 S.Ct. 1235 (2010)

In October 2009, the Supreme Court agreed to review a ruling by a three-judge panel of the D.C. Circuit Court of Appeals in the case of *Kiyemba v. Obama*, discussed *infra*. The *Kiyemba* case involved several Guantanamo detainees who, despite no longer being considered enemy combatants and having been cleared for release, had not been transferred from Guantanamo on account of the government being unable to effectuate their release to a foreign country. The *Kiyemba* petitioners sought reversal of a D.C. Circuit ruling finding that a federal habeas court lacked the authority to compel the executive to release the detainees into the United States. Following the Supreme Court's grant of certiorari, however, several *Kiyemba* petitioners were resettled in foreign countries, and the United States was able to find countries willing to settle the remaining petitioners, although five petitioners rejected these countries' offers for resettlement. On March 1, 2010, the Supreme Court vacated the appellate court's opinion and remanded the case in light of these developments. Because the Supreme Court had granted certiorari on the understanding that no remedy was available for the petitioners other than release into the United States, it returned the case to the D.C. Circuit to review the ramifications of the new circumstances. Discussion of subsequent action taken by the D.C. Circuit, as well as by the Supreme Court with respect to another petition for certiorari by the *Kiyemba* petitioners, is found below.

Kiyemba v. Obama, 131 S. Ct. 1631 (2011)

Following the Supreme Court's remand of the *Kiyemba* case back to the D.C. Circuit, the circuit panel reinstated its opinion with slight modifications. The *Kiyemba* petitioners once again sought Supreme Court review of the circuit court's ruling that federal habeas courts lacked authority to compel the petitioners' release into the United States. On April 18, 2011, the Supreme Court denied their request for review. Eight Supreme Court Justices took part in the decision, with Justice Kagan recusing herself. In joining the opinion, Justice Breyer issued a statement joined by Justices Kennedy, Ginsburg, and Sotomayor, which emphasized that the issue that had initially been presented when the *Kiyemba* petitioners first sought review by the Supreme Court was "whether a district court may order the release of an unlawfully held prisoner into the United States *where no other remedy is available*." Because the government had received offers of resettlement for the petitioners, the petitioners had not proffered or alleged evidence that they would face torture or other harm, and the government continued to seek plaintiffs' resettlement, Justice Breyer found "no Government-imposed obstacle to petitioners' timely release and appropriate resettlement." However, Justice Breyer stated that should these circumstances materially change, the petitioners "may of course raise their original issue (or related issues) again in the lower courts and in this Court."

Rulings by the D.C. Circuit Court of Appeals

Most judicial activity concerning U.S. detention policy in the conflict with Al Qaeda has occurred within the D.C. Circuit. Following the Supreme Court's ruling in *Boumediene* that the constitutional writ of habeas corpus extends to detainees held at Guantanamo, over 200 habeas petitions were filed by detainees in the U.S. District Court for the District of Columbia. Courts considering habeas claims have sometimes reached differing conclusions regarding the scope of the Executive's detention authority; the admissibility of hearsay evidence and involuntary statements made by detainees; the appropriate methodology for assessing the sufficiency and reliability of evidence proffered by the government to justify the legality of a habeas petitioner's detention; and the remedy available for those persons whom a habeas court determines to have been unlawfully detained.[16] Decisions by the U.S. Court of Appeals for the D.C. Circuit have generally been favorable to the legal positions advanced by the government. Since 2009, the appellate court has issued rulings concluding, among other things, that:

- the Executive may lawfully detain persons who are "part of" Al Qaeda, the Taliban, and affiliated groups, and possibly also persons who provide a sufficient degree of support to such entities in their hostilities against the United States and its allies (*Al-Bihani v. Obama*);

- a functional approach is appropriate when assessing whether a person is "part of" Al Qaeda, meaning that judges should consider the significance of a person's activities in relation to the organization, rather than requiring formal proof of membership, such as evidence the petitioner received orders from the organization's hierarchy (*Awad v. Obama, Bensayah v. Obama, Salahi v. Obama*);

- the government may satisfy its evidentiary burden in support of a person's detention when its factual claims are supported by a preponderance of evidence (*Al-Bihani v. Obama, Al Odah v. United States*), but a lower standard might be constitutionally permissible (*Al-Adahi v. Obama, Almerfedi v. Obama*);

- it is proper for a habeas court to assess the cumulative weight and effect of proffered evidence according to a "conditional probability analysis" when determining whether the government has demonstrated factual grounds for detaining a habeas petitioner (*Al-Adahi v. Obama, Salahi v. Obama*);

- consideration of hearsay evidence in habeas cases is not determined by the Federal Rules of Evidence (*Al Odah v. United States, Al-Madhwani v. Obama*);

- official government records, including government intelligence reports, are entitled to a presumption of regularity in Guantanamo habeas litigation (*Latif v. Obama*);

- the writ of habeas affords Guantanamo detainees with a limited right to challenge their proposed transfer to the custody of a foreign government (*Kiyemba II*);

- habeas courts lack authority, absent an authorizing statute, to compel the Executive to release non-citizen detainees into the United States, even if such persons have been determined by the court to be unlawfully detained (*Kiyemba I and III*);

- it is unlikely that noncitizens who have been transferred to foreign custody may seek judicial review of their designation as enemy combatants by the U.S. government (*Gul v. Obama*); and

---

[16] *See generally* Benjamin Wittes, Robert Chesney & Rabea Benhalim, *The Emerging Law of Detention: The Guantánamo Habeas Cases as Lawmaking*, Brookings Institute, January 22, 2010, available at http://www.brookings.edu/papers/2010/0122_guantanamo_wittes_chesney.aspx (discussing different approaches taken by district courts in the handling of habeas petitions brought by Guantanamo detainees); Wittes, Chesney, & Larkin Reynolds, *The Emerging Law of Detention 2.0: The Guantánamo Habeas Cases as Lawmaking*, Brookings Institute, May 2011, available at http://www.brookings.edu/papers/2011/05_guantanamo_wittes.aspx (discussing more recent trends in Guantanamo habeas cases, including the effects that appellate rulings have had upon habeas litigation).

- the constitutional writ of habeas does not presently extend to noncitizen detainees held at U.S.-operated facilities in Afghanistan (*Maqaleh v. Gates*).

In some of these cases, affected detainees have requested Supreme Court review. Several of these requests have been denied. It remains to be seen whether the Supreme Court will ultimately agree to review any of the D.C. Circuit's decisions, or whether the appellate court's rulings will remain controlling for the foreseeable future.

The following section discusses major rulings made by the D.C. Circuit Court of Appeals regarding persons designated as enemy combatants that involve matters of continuing relevance to U.S. detention policy. It does not discuss those rulings that were subsequently overruled by the Supreme Court on the merits.

Scope of Executive's Detention Authority and Related Evidentiary Burdens

The D.C. Circuit has issued several opinions relating to the scope of the Executive's authority to detain persons as part of the conflict with Al Qaeda, the Taliban, and associated forces. These opinions have also addressed the issues related to the sufficiency and reliability of evidence proffered by the government in support of its factual claims.

Al-Bihani v. Obama, 590 F.3d 866, *en banc rehearing denied*, 619 F.3d 1 (D.C. Cir. 2010), *cert. denied*, 131 S. Ct. 1814 (2011)

In January 2010, a three-judge panel of the D.C. Circuit Court of Appeals issued a ruling concerning the scope of the government's detention authority under the AUMF in the case of *Al-Bihani v. Obama*. In an opinion supported in full by two members of the panel,[17] the appellate court recognized that, at a minimum, the President was authorized to detain persons who were subject to the jurisdiction of military commissions established pursuant to the Military Commissions Acts of 2006 and 2009; namely, any person who was "part of forces associated with Al Qaeda or the Taliban," along with "those who purposefully and materially support such forces in hostilities against U.S. Coalition partners."[18] While the panel concluded that either purposeful and material support for an AUMF-targeted organization in hostilities against the United States or membership in such an organization may be independently sufficient to justify detention, the court declined "to explore the outer bounds of what constitutes sufficient support or indicia of membership to meet the detention standard." It did, however, note that this standard would permit the detention of a "civilian contractor" who "purposefully and materially supported" an AUMF-targeted organization through "traditional food operations essential to a fighting force and the carrying of arms."[19] Notwithstanding the government's reliance on the law of war to interpret the

---

[17] A third member of the panel issued a separate opinion concurring with the majority's judgment. However, the opinion did not clearly endorse the majority's view as to the scope of the executive's detention authority. *See* Al-Bihani v. Obama, 590 F.3d 866, 883-885 (D.C. Cir. 2010) (Williams, J., concurring) (arguing that petitioner was detainable on account of being "part of" an AUMF-targeted organization, but not deciding whether a person could be detained on account of "support" for a targeted organization that he was not also a "part of").

[18] *Id.* at 872 (quoting 2006 MCA, P.L. 109-366, §3, and 2009 MCA, P.L. 111-84, Div A, §1802).

[19] *Id.* at 872-873. The panel found that even if petitioner was not a member of an AUMF-targeted organization, his service as a cook for a military brigade affiliated with Taliban and Al Qaeda forces, in addition to his accompaniment (continued...)

scope of the AUMF and arguably in conflict with Supreme Court discussion of the issue in *Hamdi*, the panel rejected the idea that the international law of war has any relevance to the courts' interpretation of the scope of the detention power conferred by the AUMF.

The panel also held that the procedural protections afforded in habeas cases involving wartime detainees do not need to mirror those provided to persons in the traditional criminal law context, where evidence must demonstrate guilt beyond reasonable doubt, or the lesser procedures courts have used in any specific habeas context. The panel stated:

> [C]ourts are neither bound by the procedural limits created for other detention contexts nor obliged to use them as baselines from which any departures must be justified. Detention of aliens outside the sovereign territory of the United States during wartime is a different and peculiar circumstance, and the appropriate habeas procedures cannot be conceived of as mere extensions of an existing doctrine. Rather, those procedures are a whole new branch of the tree.[20]

In the context of military detention of enemy belligerents, the court found, the government need only support its authority to detain using a "preponderance of evidence" standard.[21] The court rejected the petitioner's argument, based on his reading of *Hamdi*,[22] that any relaxation of procedural standards must be justified by the particular exigencies of the case. The court established the hearsay rule for detainee habeas cases, at least those brought by aliens abroad[23]:

> [T]he question a habeas court must ask when presented with hearsay is not whether it is admissible—it is always admissible—but what probative weight to ascribe to whatever indicia of reliability it exhibits.[24]

The D.C. Circuit Court of Appeals thereafter denied a petition for an *en banc* rehearing of the *Al-Bihani* case. However, a concurring opinion joined by a majority of the active appellate court judges characterized certain aspects of the panel's decision, concerning the application of international law of war principles in interpreting the AUMF, to be non-binding dicta.[25] It did not address whether any portions of the *Al-Bihani* ruling concerning the lawfulness of detaining persons on account of membership or support for Al Qaeda, the Taliban, or associated forces also constituted non-binding dicta. However, circuit court decisions since *Al-Bihani* have appeared to construe the AUMF as authorizing the Executive to detain persons who are "part of" organizations targeted by the AUMF as well as those who provide support to such entities.[26]

(...continued)
of the brigade during military operations, constituted sufficient grounds for his detention. *Id.*

[20] Al-Bihani v. Obama, 590 F.3d 866, 877 (D.C. Cir. 2010).

[21] The preponderance standard is generally interpreted to require that the evidence presented by both sides taken together makes the facts in question more likely true than not. *See* 29 AM. JUR. 2d Evid. §173.

[22] *See* Hamdi v. Rumsfeld, 542 U.S. 507, 533-34 (2004) (O'Connell, J., plurality opinion) ("exigencies of the circumstances may demand" that procedural rules be tailored to avoid undue burden on the government, and that hearsay "may need to be accepted as the most reliable available evidence from the Government").

[23] The court distinguished the petitioner's case from any case involving a U.S. citizen or one in which an alien is detained within the United States, suggesting it might reach a different conclusion in such a case. *Al-Bihani*, 590 F.3d at 877.

[24] *Id.* at 879.

[25] Al-Bihani v. Obama, 619 F.3d 1 (D.C. Cir. 2010) (Sentelle, C.J., concurring).

[26] *See, e.g.*, Almerfedi v. Obama, 654 F.3d 1, 4 n.2 (D.C. Cir. 2011) ("As we have explained [in *Al-Bihani*], the government may detain any individual 'engaged in hostilities ... against the United States,' who 'purposefully and (continued...)

Moreover, the 2012 NDAA expressly authorizes the detention of persons who have "substantially supported al-Qaeda, the Taliban, or associated forces that are engaged in hostilities against the United States or its coalition partners, including any person who has...directly supported such hostilities in aid of such enemy forces."[27]

In any event, in litigation following *Al-Bihani* involving Guantanamo detainees, the Obama Administration has not justified its detention claims solely on the grounds that a particular detainee provided support to Al Qaeda or the Taliban. Instead, its legal justification for holding persons on account of wartime activity has been that they were at least functionally "part of" Al Qaeda, the Taliban, or an associated force at the time of capture.

On April 4, 2011, the Supreme Court denied a petition to review the *Al-Bihani* decision. The case should not be confused with ongoing litigation in a similarly-named case involving the petitioner's brother.[28] The habeas petitioner in that case has sought Supreme Court review of the denial of his habeas petition, but the Court has yet to decide whether to hear the case.

Al-Adahi v. Obama, 613 F.3d 1102 (D.C. Cir. 2010), *cert. denied*, 131 S. Ct. 1001 (2011)

In *Al-Adahi*, a three-judge panel of the D.C. Circuit endorsed the use of "conditional probability analysis" by habeas courts when considering the sufficiency and reliability of evidence proffered by the government in support of its claim that a person is lawfully detained under the AUMF. The case involved review of a district court decision granting a habeas petition by a Guantanamo detainee who the government claimed was "part of" Al Qaeda, following its determination that the government had failed to demonstrate its claim by a preponderance of evidence.

On appeal, the D.C. Circuit panel assumed *arguendo* that the government was required to show by a preponderance of evidence that the petitioner was lawfully detained under the AUMF, but suggested that reliance on this standard may not be constitutionally required. It next turned to the district court's analysis of evidence proffered by the government in support of its detention of petitioner, and concluded that the lower court "clearly erred in its treatment of the evidence" and its application of the preponderance of evidence standard. Examining the record, the circuit panel held that the lower court erred by separately considering the sufficiency of each item of evidence proffered by the government, and finding that the government failed to meet its evidentiary burden because no individual piece of evidence provided sufficient grounds to justify the petitioner's detention. The circuit panel was also critical of the lower court for failing to make any findings regarding the petitioner's "implausible" and inconsistent explanations for some of his activities, stating that it is a "well-settled principle that false exculpatory statements are evidence—often strong evidence—of guilt."

(...continued)

materially supported hostilities against the United States or its coalition partners,' or who 'is part of the Taliban, al Qaeda, or associated forces.'"); Hatim v. Gates, 632 F.3d 720 (D.C. Cir. 2011) (per curiam panel decision) (finding that district court ruling that military could only detain person who was "part of" Al Qaeda or the Taliban was "directly contrary to *Al-Bihani v. Obama*, which held that 'those who purposefully and materially support' al-Qaida or the Taliban could also be detained").

[27] 2012 NDAA, P.L. 112-81, §1021(b).

[28] Al Bihani v. Obama, No. 10-5352, 2011 U.S. App. LEXIS 2600 (D.C. Cir., February 11, 2011) (summarily affirming lower court's denial of habeas petition).

According to the circuit panel, "conditional probability analysis" is appropriate for assessing whether a person's detention under the AUMF is supported by the preponderance of the evidence. Using this framework, a habeas court must consider the cumulative weight and effect of proffered evidence when assessing whether the government has satisfied its evidentiary burden. In describing "conditional probability analysis" and its implications for the assessment of the evidence in the case before it, the *Al-Adahi* panel wrote:

> "Many mundane mistakes in reasoning can be traced to a shaky grasp of the notion of conditional probability." JOHN ALLEN PAULOS, INNUMERACY: MATHEMATICAL ILLITERACY AND ITS CONSEQUENCES 63 (1988). The key consideration is that although some events are independent (coin flips, for example), other events are dependent: "the occurrence of one of them makes the occurrence of the other more or less likely...." JOHN ALLEN PAULOS, BEYOND NUMERACY: RUMINATIONS OF A NUMBERS MAN 189 (1991). Dr. Paulos gives this example: "the probability that a person chosen at random from the phone book is over 250 pounds is quite small. However, if it's known that the person chosen is over six feet four inches tall, then the conditional probability that he or she also weighs more than 250 pounds is considerably higher." INNUMERACY 63.
>
> Those who do not take into account conditional probability are prone to making mistakes in judging evidence. They may think that if a particular fact does not itself prove the ultimate proposition (e.g., whether the detainee was part of al-Qaida), the fact may be tossed aside and the next fact may be evaluated as if the first did not exist. This is precisely how the district court proceeded in this case: Al-Adahi's ties to bin Laden "cannot prove" he was part of Al-Qaida and this evidence therefore "must not distract the Court." ... The fact that Al-Adahi stayed in an al-Qaida guesthouse "is not in itself sufficient to justify detention." Al-Adahi's attendance at an al-Qaida training camp "is not sufficient to carry the Government's burden of showing that he was a part" of al-Qaida. And so on. The government is right: the district court wrongly "required each piece of the government's evidence to bear weight without regard to all (or indeed any) other evidence in the case. This was a fundamental mistake that infected the court's entire analysis."[29]

Employing this standard, the circuit panel examined the evidentiary record (including false exculpatory statements made by the petitioner during interrogation),[30] and concluded that the government had satisfied its evidentiary burden of proving that the petitioner was subject to detention on account of membership in Al Qaeda. The circuit panel also concluded that some of the individual pieces of evidence proffered by the government—including evidence showing that the petitioner had voluntarily stayed at an Al Qaeda guesthouse and had received and executed orders from Al Qaeda members while at a weapons training camp—constituted sufficient grounds to justify his detention.

On January 18, 2011, the Supreme Court denied a petition of certiorari to review the *Al-Adahi* ruling.

---

[29] Al-Adahi v. Obama, 613 F.3d 1102, 1105-1106 (D.C. Cir. 2010) (omitting some citations contained in original

[30] In support of its finding that the government had demonstrated by a preponderance of evidence that the petitioner was a member of Al Qaeda, the circuit panel cited, *inter alia,* evidence relating to the petitioner's travel to Afghanistan in 2001, his subsequent meetings with Osama Bin Laden, his stay at an Al Qaeda guesthouse, his presence at an Al Qaeda-affiliated training camp, and his wearing of a watch at the time of capture that was of the same model as that used by Al Qaeda operatives.

Awad v. Obama, 608 F.3d 1 (D.C. Cir. 2010), *cert. denied*, 131 S. Ct. 1814 (2011)

This case involved the review of a district court's denial of habeas relief to a Guantanamo detainee whom the government alleged to have been "part of" Al Qaeda at the time of capture. The petitioner, a Yemeni national, admitted to U.S. interrogators that he had travelled to Afghanistan to receive weapons training and fight U.S. forces. He was subsequently injured in an air raid, which resulted in the amputation of one of his legs. When Al Qaeda took over a portion of a hospital where petitioner was being treated, he allegedly joined Al Qaeda fighters barricaded there when coalition forces attempted to re-take the hospital, but he was surrendered by Al Qaeda fighters due to his injury.

In upholding the district court's denial of habeas relief, the circuit panel rejected several legal and factual challenges raised by petitioner. As an initial matter, the *Awad* panel reaffirmed the propriety of using conditional probability analysis, previously relied upon by the D.C. Circuit in *Al-Adahi*, to assess petitioner's evidentiary challenges; accordingly, it would not "weigh each piece of evidence in isolation, but [would] consider all of the evidence taken as a whole." The circuit panel then proceeded to consider petitioner's argument that some of the evidence that had been proffered against him, including Al Qaeda documents and out-of-court statements by another detainee who was present at the hospital where petitioner was apprehended, were unreliable hearsay. The panel noted past jurisprudence recognizing that "hearsay evidence is admissible in this type of habeas proceeding if the hearsay is reliable," and concluded that the proffered evidence was sufficiently reliable to have been considered by the lower court.

The court then turned to petitioner's legal challenges. The panel rejected petitioner's argument the government was required to justify its claims that he was lawfully detainable through clear and convincing evidence, and found that the less rigorous "preponderance of evidence" standard that had been relied upon by the district court was constitutionally permissible. The circuit panel also dismissed petitioner's argument that his habeas petition could only be denied if a specific finding of fact was made that petitioner would pose a threat to the United States and its allies if released. The panel characterized the circuit court's prior decision in *Al-Bihani* as foreclosing this argument, and it went on to state that

> the United States's authority to detain an enemy combatant is not dependent on whether an individual would pose a threat ... if released but rather upon the continuation of hostilities.... Whether a detainee would pose a threat to U.S. interests if released is not at issue in habeas corpus proceedings in federal courts concerning aliens detained under the authority conferred by the AUMF.

Finally, the panel rejected petitioner's argument that, in order for the government to justify his detention under the AUMF, it would have to demonstrate that he was part of Al Qaeda's "command structure." The panel held that petitioner's actions in joining Al Qaeda fighters behind a barricade were sufficient grounds to conclude he was "part of" Al Qaeda. It also suggested other situations where the government would not need to prove that a detainee was subject to Al Qaeda's "command structure" in order to justify its conclusion that he was "part of" Al Qaeda, such as when a person was captured in Afghanistan as part of a group that was shooting at U.S. forces and identified himself upon capture as an Al Qaeda member.

The Supreme Court denied a petition to review the *Awad* decision on April 4, 2011.

Al Odah v. United States, 611 F.3d 8 (D.C. Cir. 2010), cert. denied, 131 S. Ct. 1812 (2011)

In June 2010, a three-judge panel of the D.C. Circuit Court of Appeals upheld a district court's denial of a habeas petition brought on behalf of a person who had been detained at Guantanamo since 2002 due to his allegedly being part of Al Qaeda and Taliban forces. The petitioner challenged the procedures used by the district court when admitting evidence, and also the sufficiency of the evidence upon which its judgment on the merits was based. The circuit panel rejected these challenges as being foreclosed by controlling legal precedent. Specifically, the panel rejected the petitioner's argument that the government was required to support its factual claims in support of the legality of the petitioner's detention through "clear and convincing evidence." The panel recognized that based on binding precedent within the circuit, it is "well-settled law that a preponderance of the evidence standard is constitutional in considering a habeas petition from an individual detained pursuant to authority granted by the AUMF."

The panel further rejected petitioner's argument that the admission of hearsay was statutorily restricted by the Federal Rules of Evidence and federal habeas statute. The court found this argument unpersuasive, citing both to the Supreme Court's ruling in *Hamdi* and the appellate court's prior jurisprudence as recognizing that district courts may admit reliable hearsay evidence when considering a habeas petition by an individual detained under the AUMF. In this case, the court agreed with the lower court that the hearsay evidence demonstrated sufficient indicia of reliability to be accorded weight:

> For example, in considering interrogation reports of a third party concerning al Qaeda and Taliban travel routes into Afghanistan, the [district] court noted that this hearsay was corroborated by "multiple other examples of individuals who used this route to travel to Afghanistan for the purpose of jihad." The court indicated that it was aware of the limitations of this evidence when it concluded that "[although far from conclusive, the Government's evidence suggests that an individual using this travel route to reach Kandahar may have done so because it was a route used by some individuals seeking to enter Afghanistan for the purpose of jihad."[31]

The court approved this analysis of hearsay and declined to find an abuse of discretion on the part of the district court. The panel also rejected the petitioner's challenges to the individual pieces of evidence proffered by the government in support of his detention.

On April 4, 2011, the Supreme Court denied a petition to review the *Al-Odah* decision. The *Al-Odah* ruling has been relied upon by the D.C. Circuit in other cases, including in at least one case where which a petition for certiorari has been filed with the Supreme Court but a ruling has yet to be made.[32]

---

[31] Al Odah v. United States, 611 F.3d 8, 14 (D.C. Cir. 2010) (citing 648 F. Supp. 2d 1, 10 (D.D.C. 2009)).

[32] Al Kandari v. United States, No. 10-5373, 2011 U.S. App. LEXIS 24656 (December 11, 2011) (in an unpublished opinion, ruling that petitioner's argument that the Federal Rules of Evidence applied to Guantanamo habeas litigation was foreclosed by *Al-Odah*).

Bensayah v. Obama, 610 F.3d 718 (D.C. Cir. 2010)

This case involved the review of a district court denial of habeas relief to an Algerian citizen who had been arrested by Bosnian authorities in 2001 and was subsequently transferred to U.S. custody for detention at Guantanamo. The government claimed that although the petitioner had not directly taken part in combat activities against the United States, he had intended to travel to Afghanistan to fight U.S. forces and had facilitated the travel of others to do the same. The executive branch initially argued that it had legal authority to hold the detainee, pursuant to the authority vested by the AUMF and the President's "inherent authority" as Commander-in-Chief, on account of the detainee's alleged membership in and support for Al Qaeda. In 2008, a federal district court judge denied the detainee's habeas petition.[33] The court found that the government had sufficient grounds to detain the petitioner for providing support to Al Qaeda, but declined to decide whether there were also sufficient grounds to detain the petitioner for being "part of" the organization.

On appeal, the executive eschewed reliance on certain evidence that it earlier relied upon to demonstrate that petitioner acted as a travel facilitator for Al Qaeda, and also modified its argument in support of petitioner's detention—abandoning its argument that the petitioner was subject to detention on account of providing support to Al Qaeda, and instead arguing that he was subject to detention on account of being "part of" the organization. The government also relied solely on the authority granted by the AUMF to justify its detention authority, rather than any independent authority deriving from the Commander-in-Chief Clause. The reviewing circuit panel reversed and remanded the case back to the district court, finding that evidence relied upon by the lower court to conclude that the petitioner had supported Al Qaeda was insufficient to show that he was "part of" the organization.

Portions of the appellate panel's opinion discussing the sufficiency and reliability of the evidence proffered by the government were largely redacted. However, the published opinion provided further clarification regarding the D.C. Circuit's view of the detention authority conferred by the AUMF. The *Bensayah* panel recognized that the D.C. Circuit had previously made clear that "the AUMF authorizes the Executive to detain, at the least, any individual who is functionally part of al Qaeda." According to the panel, because Al Qaeda's organizational structure is generally unknown and thought to be amorphous, a determination as to whether an individual is "part of" the organization "must be made on a case-by-case basis by using a functional rather than a formal approach and by focusing upon the actions of the individual in relation to the organization." Although the panel concluded that evidence demonstrating that a person operated within Al Qaeda's command structure was sufficient to show that he was "part of" the organization, it suggested that there "may be other indicia that a particular individual is sufficiently involved with the organization to be deemed part of it." Nonetheless, the panel indicated that the "purely independent conduct of a freelancer" is not sufficient grounds to deem him to be functionally part of Al Qaeda.

Salahi v. Obama, 625 F.3d 745 (D.C. Cir. 2010)

This case involved review of a district court order granting habeas relief to a Guantanamo detainee captured in 2001 in Mauritania. Although the petitioner had not fought against the United States, the government alleged that he was lawfully detained on the grounds that he was

---

[33] Boumediene v. Bush, 579 F. Supp. 2d 191 (D.D.C. 2008).

"part of" Al Qaeda. Most of the evidence proffered by the government in support of its allegations concerned activities by the petitioner which occurred years before the 9/11 attacks. In habeas proceedings before the lower court, the government presented evidence that petitioner swore an oath of loyalty to Al Qaeda in 1991 and provided support to the organization at various points thereafter, including by recruiting members, hosting organization leaders, and providing the organization with financial support. For his part, the petitioner claimed that he severed ties with Al Qaeda in the early 1990s. The district court ruled that the government failed to satisfy its evidentiary burden in proving that the petitioner was "part of" Al Qaeda at the time of capture, and ordered the detainee to be released. In doing so, it rejected the government's argument that once the petitioner swore an oath of allegiance to Al Qaeda, he bore the burden of demonstrating that he had later withdrawn from the organization.

On appeal, a three-judge panel vacated the lower court's decision, finding that intervening case law—namely, the circuit court's opinions in the *Al-Adahi*, *Awad*, and *Bensayah* cases discussed above—cast doubt on the lower court's approach to determining whether petitioner was "part of" Al Qaeda. In particular, the *Salahi* panel found that the lower court had improperly required the government to prove that the petitioner had received and executed orders from Al Qaeda in order to demonstrate his membership in the organization. Subsequent circuit jurisprudence established that membership could be demonstrated not only from evidence that a person was part of Al Qaeda's "command structure," but also from activities which revealed a person to be functionally part of the organization. The panel recognized, however, that in cases like the one involving petitioner, who had not engaged in combat activities against the United States, "the government's failure to prove that an individual was acting under orders from al-Qaida may be *relevant* to the question of whether the individual was 'part of' the organization when captured."[34]

Although the government requested that the *Salahi* panel direct the district court to deny the habeas petition, it declined to do so, finding that it was appropriate to remand the case so the lower court could conduct further proceedings consistent with circuit jurisprudence that developed after its initial ruling. The panel found that because the lower court lacked guidance from subsequent circuit jurisprudence, it had primarily looked for evidence as to whether petitioner participated in Al Qaeda's command structure, but "did not make definitive findings regarding certain key facts necessary for us to determine as a matter of law whether Salahi was in fact 'part of' al-Qaida when captured."

In remanding the case to the lower court for further factual findings, the *Salahi* panel reiterated the admonition made by the circuit court in *Al-Adahi* that courts considering habeas petitions by Guantanamo detainees must consider the assorted evidence relating to the government's claims collectively rather than in isolation. While the panel stated that the lower court appeared to have generally followed this approach, it suggested that its consideration of certain evidence "may have been unduly atomized." Notably, the panel suggested that when the lower court determined that the petitioner's limited relationships with Al Qaeda operatives might have been too insubstantial to independently serve as a basis for deeming the petitioner "part of" Al Qaeda, those connections made it more probable that the petitioner was a member of the organization and were thus relevant to an assessment as to whether he had been lawfully detained. The panel also suggested that examining the petitioner's oath to Al Qaeda in isolation from his subsequent "sporadic support" may have resulted in the lower court failing to consider the possibility that this support demonstrated the petitioner's continued adherence to his oath of loyalty.

---

[34] Salahi v. Obama, 625 F.3d 745, 752 (D.C. Cir. 2010) (italics in original).

In reaching its ruling, the appellate court did not squarely address the government's argument that the petitioner's oath to Al Qaeda in the early 1990s established an evidentiary burden upon him to demonstrate that he had subsequently withdrawn from the organization. The appellate court also declined to consider the government's argument that the district court had accorded insufficient weight to certain inculpatory statements that were made by petitioner in interrogations subsequent to a period of time when he had been, by the government's admission, subject to mistreatment, because the panel viewed this issue to be irrelevant to the legal questions addressed by its opinion conditional probability analysis.

Uthman v. Obama, 637 F.3d 400 (D.C. Cir. 2011)

In *Uthman*, a three-judge circuit panel reversed and remanded a district court decision that had granted habeas relief to a Yemeni national who had been captured in Afghanistan and detained by U.S. forces since December 2001. In prior cases, including the *Bensayah* and *Salahi* decisions discussed *supra*, the D.C. Circuit had recognized that the determination of whether a person was "part of" Al Qaeda was based on a functional, case-by-case assessment which focused on the individual's actions in relation to the organization. The *Uthman* decision provided further clarification as to the kind of circumstantial evidence that could potentially provide sufficient grounds to support the detention of a person under the AUMF.

The government made several claims regarding Uthman's activities in relation to Al Qaeda – including that he attended an Al Qaeda training camp, fought against the Northern Alliance in Afghanistan, and served as a bodyguard to Osama Bin Laden – which were contested. Nonetheless, the D.C. Circuit panel found that the following facts, which were either found by the district court or which were uncontested by Uthman, were sufficient to demonstrate that Uthman was "more likely than not" part of Al Qaeda and therefore subject to detention: (1) he was captured in December of 2001 in the vicinity of Tora Bora, where Al Qaeda forces had gathered to fight United States and its allies; (2) at the time of capture, Uthman was travelling with a small group including two Al Qaeda members who were bodyguards for Osama Bin Laden and a Taliban fighter; (3) he had previously studied at a religious school in Yemen which was known as "a fruitful al Qaeda recruiting ground," and which had also been attended by the Al Qaeda and Taliban fighters with whom Uthman had been captured; (4) Uthman's travel route to Afghanistan resembled that commonly used by Al Qaeda recruits; (5) his explanation for how he raised funds to travel to Afghanistan was not viewed as credible by the district court, and constituted a "false exculpatory" statement lending credence to the government's claims of wrongdoing; (6) Uthman was seen at an al Qaeda guesthouse; and (7) Uthman's exculpatory explanation of his activities in Pakistan and Afghanistan involved "many coincidences that are perhaps possible, but not likely." Although the panel recognized that at least some of these findings, when viewed in isolation, would not necessarily be sufficient to find that Uthman was functionally part of Al Qaeda, it ruled that when the evidence proffered by the government was considered in totality, "Uthman's actions and recurrent entanglement with al Qaeda show that he more likely than not was part of al Qaeda."

Uthman has filed a petition requesting Supreme Court review of the circuit decision, but the Court has not yet decided whether to grant or deny the petition.

Al-Madhwani v. Obama, 642 F.3d 1071 (D.C. Cir. 2011)

In *Al-Madhwani*, a three-judge appellate panel reviewed and affirmed a lower court dismissal of a habeas petition by a Guantanamo detainee. Madhwani argued that the government provided insufficient evidence to demonstrate that he was subject to detention under the AUMF, and also alleged that the district court had improperly considered evidence outside the record and had committed procedural errors. The petitioner also claimed that he had been tortured by U.S. authorities prior to his transfer to Guantanamo, and argued that statements he made to military authorities at Guantanamo were tainted by his earlier coercion.

In upholding the district court's denial of habeas, the circuit panel found it unnecessary to reach Madhwani's challenge that certain evidence had been tainted by undue coercion, as there was sufficient evidence untainted by these claims to support the district court's decision. The panel noted that the district court had considered 260 exhibits and held a four-day merits hearing during which petitioner himself testified for over one day, and discounted "a substantial portion" of the government's evidence based on a finding that it was tainted by mistreatment suffered by petitioner prior to his transfer to Guantanamo. The panel found the evidence considered by the lower court, including incriminating testimony by Madhwani in testimony, provided sufficient grounds to support the government's determination that he was "part of" Al Qaeda. This evidence included admissions by Madhwani of his stay at an Al Qaeda-affiliated guest house and military training camp; his admission to carrying a rifle at the behest of camp superiors, his "suspicious" travel after departing the camp with recruits and "implausible" explanation for his travel; and the circumstances of his final capture in the company of at least one known Al Qaeda operative.

The panel also rejected several other legal and evidentiary arguments made by Madhwani, including certain arguments that had been previously rejected by the D.C. Circuit, including his claim that hearsay evidence could only be admitted in wartime detention cases if it fell within an exception recognized under the Federal Rules of Evidence.

A petition for certiorari has been filed in *Al-Madhwani*, but the Supreme Court has yet to decide whether to hear the case.

Almerfedi v. Obama, 654 F.3d 1 (D.C. Cir. 2011)

In *Almerfedi*, a three-judge panel of the D.C. Circuit considered the government's appeal of a district court ruling granting habeas relief to a Guantanamo detainee whom the government claimed had acted as a facilitator for Al Qaeda. The government based its claim primarily upon admissions made by habeas petitioner Almerfedi himself, as well as statements made by another Guantanamo detainee. The district court concluded, however, that Almerfedi's statements did not demonstrate by a preponderance of the evidence that Almerfedi was "part of" Al Qaeda. It also declined to consider the testimony of the fellow Guantanamo detainee, concluding that it was unreliable. The circuit panel reversed and remanded with instructions to the lower court to deny Almerfedi's habeas petition.

The circuit court's ruling did not clearly pronounce any new legal standards governing consideration of detainees' habeas claims (though the majority opinion reiterated the suggestion made in *Al-Adahi* that the government might be able to support the detention of a person using a lower standard than one based on the preponderance of evidence).[35] However, some have viewed the decision as significant because the court implied that the government's evidence was not as compelling as evidence proffered in prior cases reviewed by the D.C. Circuit, and might signify "the minimum amount of evidence" necessary to demonstrate under a preponderance of evidence standard that an individual was lawfully detained.[36]

The government's contention that Almerfedi served as a facilitator for Al Qaeda was based on several factors. By Almerfedi's own admission, he had travelled from Yemen to Pakistan in 2001, where he stayed for more than two months at the headquarters of Jama'at Tablighi, an Islamic missionary organization designated by U.S. intelligence as a Terrorist Support Entity closely aligned with Al Qaeda. He subsequently travelled to Iran, where he admitted staying for over a month before being arrested by Iranian authorities with at least $2,000 cash in his possession. The government further claimed, based on statements Almerfedi allegedly made to another Guantanamo detainee named al-Jadani, that while Almerfedi was in Iran he stayed at an Al Qaeda guest house in Tehran. Al-Jadani also claimed that other, unnamed Guantanamo detainees had informed him that a "Hussain al-Aden" acted as an Al Qaeda facilitator at the Tehran guesthouse, and the government believed that "Hussain al-Adeni was the same person as Almerfedi because the *nisha* 'al-Adeni' means 'from Aden,' which is [the Yemeni city] where Almerfedi is from."[37]

For his part, Almerfedi denied that he had ever stayed at an Al Qaeda guesthouse or served as a facilitator, and noted that the dates when al-Jadani claimed he stayed at the guesthouse were obviously incorrect, because it was undisputed that Almerfedi had been arrested by Iranian authorities at least a year earlier. Almerfedi alleged that he had left Yemen in order to seek a better life in Europe. He claimed to have travelled to Pakistan because it would be easier to obtain a visa there, and that he stayed with Jama'at Tablighi in the hope that he could take advantage of the travel discounts they offered members (even though he denied ever being a member of the organization). He further alleged that his subsequent travel to and stay in Iran were part of a failed attempt to be smuggled into Europe.

Examining the record, the circuit court concluded that "the government's evidence, combined with Almerfedi's incredible explanations" provided sufficient grounds to detain Almerfedi even without consideration of al-Jadani's statements. The court noted that Almerfedi's stay at the headquarters of Jama'at Tablighi was "probative, by itself it presumably would not be sufficient to carry the government's burden because there are surely some persons associated with Jama'at Tablighi who are not affiliated with al-Qaeda."[38] However, when this fact was considered along with Almerfedi's travel route, which the court described as being "quite at odds with his professed desire to travel to Europe," in addition to the circumstances of Almerfedi's capture with at least $2,000 of unexplained cash in his possession, the government's case that Almerfedi acted as an Al Qaeda facilitator "was on firmer ground." Further, the circuit panel found that although the lower court had recognized Almerfedi's explanation of his activities as "perplexing" and unconvincing, it erred by failing to assess these "false exculpatory statements" as amounting to evidence in favor of the government's position, as the D.C. Circuit had held in *Al-Adahi*.

---

[35] Almerfedi v. Obama, 654 F.3d 1, 5 n.4 (D.C. Cir. 2011).

[36] *Id*. at 4 (claiming that [T] the government's evidence may well have been stronger in previous cases than in this case. But that is irrelevant; all of those cases were not close.").

[37] *Id*. at 3.

[38] *Id*. at 6.

While finding that the admission of al-Jadani's statements was unnecessary for the government to satisfy the evidentiary burden justifying Almerfedi's detention, two panel members nonetheless concluded that the lower court clearly erred in ruling these statements as unreliable "jail house gossip." The district court had rejected al-Jadani's statements at least in part because al-Jadani alleged that Almerfedi told him that he was at an Al Qaeda guesthouse in 2002 or 2003, though Almerfedi had already been taken into custody by that time. The majority of the circuit panel believed, however, that al-Jadani's "timing confusions were inconsequential," because the correct date of Almerfedi's capture had been given in some reports of al-Jadani's interrogations by U.S. authorities, and al-Jadani's reliability had been established via a classified government declaration which buttressed many of his statements regarding Al Qaeda guesthouses in Iran. The majority of the panel also believed that the district court erred when it failed to assess al-Jadani's recounting of conversations with unnamed detainees that implicated Almerfedi. The panel majority viewed it as "quite understandable that al-Jadani would be reluctant" to identify these detainees to U.S. authorities. Moreover, the panel majority found it significant that al-Jadani knew specific details regarding the capture of a "Hussain al-Aden" by Iranian authorities and his subsequent transfer first to Afghan and then to U.S. custody. The panel majority characterized the circumstances as matching "Almerfedi's unique experiences and therefore mak[ing] clear that Hussain Almerfedi and Hussain al-Adeni are the same man," buttressing the credibility of al-Jadani and that of the unnamed detainees who purportedly identified Almerfedi as an Al Qaeda facilitator.

Writing separately, D.C. Circuit Judge Judith W. Rogers concurred with the panel majority in its ruling that the government had satisfied the evidentiary burden needed to support Almerfedi's detention. However, Judge Rogers disagreed with the majority's analysis of the recorded statements of al-Jadani. The district court's determination that al-Jadani's statements were unreliable was a factual one that could only be reversed for clear error, and an examination of the record evidenced did "not lead to a 'firm conviction' that the district court's analysis of al-Jadani's statements was mistaken, much less implausible."

A petition for Supreme Court review has been filed in the *Almerfedi* case, but the Court has yet to decide whether to grant an appeal of the circuit court's decision.

Al Alwi v. Obama, 653 F.3d 11 (D.C. Cir. 2011)

In this case, a circuit panel found that although the corroboration of hearsay statements has proved useful to establish their reliability, corroboration of statements made by the petitioner himself during interrogations is not necessary to find that he is lawfully detained. The district court had sustained Al Alwi's detention based on admissions he made during interrogation that established he had traveled to Afghanistan to join the fight against the Northern Alliance, had stayed in at least three guesthouses associated with enemy forces, received military training and participated in hostilities against the Northern Alliance, and was part of a unit that was bombed by U.S. forces in late 2001.[39] Al Alwi sought to have the denial of his habeas petition reversed on the basis that his statements were insufficiently corroborated by other evidence, which he argued was required under the "corroboration rule" applicable in criminal trials. The appellate court expressed skepticism that such a rule still exists in the criminal context, but regarded it as irrelevant to habeas proceedings,[40] where other indicia of reliability could satisfy the requirement

---

[39] Al Alwi v. Obama, 653 F.3d 11, 16-17 (D.C. Cir. 2011).

[40] *Id.* at 18-19.

to assess the probative value of such statements. In this case, the interrogation reports were found to be sufficiently reliable because Al Alwi's statements were consistent and he did not contend that he gave false answers during any specific session due to the coercive interrogation methods he alleged were used. Moreover, the government did submit evidence other than the petitioner's statements to demonstrate the connection between the admissions and inferences that could be drawn from them (i.e., such conduct was typical of Taliban and Al Qaeda recruits).[41]

The appellate court declined to review the petitioner's argument that his detention was no longer lawful because the "associated force" of which he was allegedly a member is no longer engaged in hostilities, stating that he had failed to raise the argument before the lower court and that there was sufficient evidence to establish he was a part of the Taliban or Al Qaeda.[42] The court also rejected Al Alwi's argument that the government must prove not only that he was "part of" Al Qaeda or the Taliban, but also that he "substantially supported" one of those entities. Although the district court had not squarely addressed whether Al Alwi was a part of any group of combatants, the appellate court found that enough facts had been established for it to make that determination on review, without remanding the case for further finding of fact. Finally, the circuit panel rejected the petitioner's contention that the district court's denial of his unopposed request for a 30-day continuance amounted to an abuse of discretion. He had asked for extra time because he had been unable to meet with his attorneys due to his having begun a hunger strike, but the court denied the request because Al Alwi was himself responsible for the delay. While the appellate court agreed that the denial of Al Alwi's request was difficult to understand in light of the fact that the district court had granted the government a similar continuance without objection, it stated that the petitioner must be able to demonstrate actual prejudice from the denial, which he had failed to do. The district judge had permitted his attorneys to submit an amended response, and at any rate, according to the panel, it could not be demonstrated that 30 days would have made an appreciable difference given the amount of time his counsel had been working with him through the CSRT and habeas proceedings.

A petition has been filed for Supreme Court review of the *Al Alwi* decision, but the Court has yet to decide whether to accept an appeal.

Latif v. Obama, 666 F.3d 746 (D.C. Cir. 2011)

In this case a three-judge circuit panel reviewed a district court ruling granting the habeas petition of a Guantanamo detainee whom the government claimed was subject to detention under the AUMF. The district court had found that the government failed to satisfy its evidentiary burden to demonstrate its allegation that Latif, a Yemeni national who had travelled to Afghanistan and was subsequently captured in Pakistan, had fought with the Taliban and was subject to detention. In a 2-1 decision, the panel vacated the district court's ruling and remanded the case for further proceedings. The panel's published decision is heavily redacted, with much of the discussion centering on classified government intelligence documents that served as the primary evidentiary basis supporting the government's allegations. The panel majority found that the district court erred by not affording a "presumption of regularity" to the intelligence documents proffered by the government, and that Latif had not presented evidence to satisfactorily rebut the presumption that the intelligence documents accurately recorded the statements made therein.

---

[41] *Id.* at 20.

[42] *Id.* at 18 n.7.

The controlling opinion in *Latif*, written by Judge Brown, described the presumption of regularity as applicable to "the official acts of public officers and, in the absence of clear evidence to the contrary, courts presume that they have properly discharged their official duties." Judge Brown distinguished a presumption of regularity from a presumption of truthfulness, and suggested that confusion over the distinction might explain the prior reluctance of lower courts to accord a presumption of regularity to government intelligence documents:

> The confusion stems from the fact that intelligence reports involve two distinct actors—the non-government source and the government official who summarizes (or transcribes) the source's statement. The presumption of regularity pertains only to the second: it presumes the government official accurately identified the source and accurately summarized his statement, but it implies nothing about the truth of the underlying non-government source's statement. There are many conceivable reasons why a government document might accurately record a statement that is itself incredible. A source may be shown to have lied, for example, or he may prove his statement was coerced. The presumption of regularity—to the extent it is not rebutted—requires a court to treat the Government's record as accurate; it does not compel a determination that the record establishes what it is offered to prove.[43]

The majority characterized the application of a presumption of regularity to intelligence documents as being supported by separation of powers principles; because "courts have no special expertise in evaluating the nature and reliability of the Executive branch's wartime record...it is appropriate to defer to Executive branch expertise."[44] The majority also noted that this presumption regularly given to government documents in other contexts, including in ordinary criminal cases. It also discussed prior D.C. Circuit rulings which it characterized as being consistent with or lending support to the panel's holding.

Reviewing the evidence before the district court, the panel majority found that the intelligence report proffered by the government, if reliable, provided sufficient evidence to demonstrate the lawfulness of Latif's detention. Because the majority held that this report was entitled to a presumption of regularity, and because Latif "challenge[d] only the reliability of the Report," the majority found that it could only uphold the district court's grant of habeas if Latif was able to rebut the government's evidence "with more convincing evidence of his own."[45] The majority found that he had not done so, and in addition, it found that the district court had failed to consider properly relevant evidence in assessing Latif's credibility, including the similarity between Latif's travel route and that commonly used by Al Qaeda and Taliban fights, as well as potentially incriminating statements that he made. The panel remanded the case back to the district court for further consideration of the evidence.

Judge Henderson wrote a separate concurrence to the panel decision, agreeing with the controlling opinion's analysis but arguing that remand was unnecessary and that the panel should have simply reversed the lower court's grant of habeas.

Writing in dissent, Judge Tatel argued that the district court's factual findings were subject to a deferential clear error standard of review, and that employing this standard would have resulted in affirming the lower court's grant of habeas. He also disputed the majority's holding that a

---

[43] Latif v. Obama, 666 F.3d 746, 750-751 (D.C. 2011)

[44] *Id.* at 751.

[45] *Id.* at 755. The panel majority expressly declined to "decide precisely how much more the detainee must show to overcome the presumption of regularity." *Id.* at 755 n5.

presumption of regularity should apply to government intelligence documents in habeas cases. He characterized the presumption as typically being applied to those government documents which are "familiar, transparent, generally understood as reliable, or accessible." Judge Tatel argued that presumption should not apply to intelligence documents of the kind at issue here, which "was produced in the fog of war by a clandestine method that we know almost nothing about." He further expressed fear that application of this presumption would in practice come "perilously close to suggesting that whatever the government says must be treated as true...."[46]

A petition has been filed for Supreme Court review of the *Latif* decision, but the Court has yet to decide whether to accept an appeal.

Transfer and Release of Detainees

The D.C. Circuit has also considered a number of cases involving issues related to the transfer or release of Guantanamo detainees. Some of these cases concern the remedy available to persons whom a reviewing court has determined to be unlawfully held, but who cannot be resettled or repatriated to a foreign country in the near future due to legal or practical obstacles.[47] Other cases involve challenges by detainees to their impending transfer to a specific foreign country, where detainees claim that they would be tortured or unlawfully detained by the government of the receiving country. The D.C. Circuit has also indicated that it is highly unlikely that a detainee may challenge his designation as an enemy combatant after being released from U.S. custody and transferred to a foreign country.

Kiyemba v. Obama, 555 F.3d 1022 (D.C. Cir. 2009) ("*Kiyemba I*"), *vacated*, 130 S. Ct. 1235 (2010), *reinstated as amended*, 605 F.3d 1046 (D.C. Cir. 2010) ("*Kiyemba III*"), *cert. denied*, 131 S. Ct. 1631 (2011)

In October 2008, a federal district court ordered the release into the United States of several Guantanamo detainees who were no longer considered enemy combatants but who could not be returned to their home country (China) because of the likelihood they would be subjected to torture there, finding that the political branches' plenary authority in the immigration context did not contravene the petitioners' entitlement to an effective remedy to their unauthorized detention.[48] However, the D.C. Circuit panel stayed the district court's order pending appellate review,[49] and subsequently reversed the district court's decision in the case of *Kiyemba v. Obama* ("*Kiyemba I*"), decided in February 2009. The majority held that although the constitutional writ of habeas enables Guantanamo detainees to challenge the legality of their detention, habeas courts lack authority (absent the enactment of an authorizing statute) to compel the transfer of a non-citizen detainee into the United States, even if that detainee is found to be unlawfully held and the government has been unable to effectuate his release to a foreign county. The *Kiyemba I* panel's decision was primarily based on long-standing jurisprudence in the immigration context which recognizes that the political branches have plenary authority over whether arriving aliens may

---

[46] *Id.* at 779 (Tatel, J., dissenting) (quoting Parhat v. Gates, 532 F.3d 834, 849 (D.C. Cir. 2008)).

[47] For discussion of U.S. policy relating to the transfer or release of Guantanamo detainees to foreign countries, see CRS Report R40139, *Closing the Guantanamo Detention Center: Legal Issues*, by Michael John Garcia et al.

[48] *In re* Guantanamo Bay Detainee Litigation, 581 F. Supp. 2d 33 (D.D.C. 2008).

[49] Kiyemba v. Bush, No. 08-5424, 2008 WL 4898963, Order (D.C. Cir., October 20, 2008) (*per curiam*).

enter the United States. The majority of the panel also found that Guantanamo detainees were not protected by the Due Process Clause of the Constitution, as they are non-citizens held outside the U.S. and lack significant ties to the country.

As discussed *supra*, the Supreme Court granted certiorari to review the *Kiyemba* ruling, and subsequently vacated the appellate court's opinion and remanded the case in light of the fact that several countries had thereafter agreed to resettle the petitioners. In May 2010, the D.C. Circuit panel reinstated its earlier opinion, as modified to take into account subsequent congressional enactments limiting the use of funds to release any Guantanamo detainee into the United States (the panel's reinstatement is commonly referred to as "*Kiyemba III*," to distinguish it from the Circuit panel's initial ruling and an intervening case also entitled *Kiyemba v. Obama*). The detainees at issue in *Kiyemba III* have filed a petition for writ of certiorari with the Supreme Court, seeking review of the circuit court's ruling.

Kiyemba v. Obama, 561 F.3d 509 (D.C. Cir. 2009) ("*Kiyemba II*"), cert. denied, 130 S.Ct. 1880 (2010)

In another case entitled *Kiyemba v. Obama* (commonly referred to as "*Kiyemba II*"), a D.C. Circuit panel considered habeas petitions by detainees who were no longer considered enemy combatants, and who sought to prevent their transfer to any country where they would likely face further detention or torture. The *Kiyemba II* panel rejected the government's argument that the MCA stripped the court of jurisdiction to hear claims related to the petitioners' proposed transfer. The panel interpreted *Boumediene* as invalidating the MCA's court-stripping provisions with respect "to all *habeas* claims brought by Guantanamo detainees, not simply with respect to so-called 'core' *habeas* claims" relating to the legality of the petitioners' detention. However, the panel held that an executive branch determination that a detainee will not be tortured if transferred to a particular country is binding on the court, and a habeas court may not second-guess this assessment. The circuit panel also reversed a district court ruling that required the government to provide 30 days' notice to detainees' counsel before any proposed transfer. As a result of this ruling, the detainees' ability to challenge their proposed transfer from Guantanamo may be quite limited. On March 22, 2010, the Supreme Court denied a petition for writ of certiorari to review the appellate court's ruling.

The *Kiyemba II* decision has been relied upon by the D.C. Circuit in subsequent rulings concerning detainees' right to challenge the executive's determination that they would not face torture if transferred to a particular country and receive advance notice of their proposed transfer. Some of these cases are the subject of ongoing litigation.

Gul v. Obama, 652 F.3d 12 (D.C. Circ. 2011)

This case involved two former Guantanamo detainees who sought to challenge their designation as "enemy combatants" by the U.S. government, despite the fact that they were no longer in U.S. custody. Following the detainees' transfer to foreign government custody, the lower court dismissed their habeas petitions as moot. The detainees appealed to the D.C. Circuit, arguing that dismissal was improper and that they had suffered collateral consequences even after leaving U.S. custody because of their enemy combatant designation.

The three-judge panel upheld the lower court's dismissal. The court held that even assuming that courts may retain habeas jurisdiction over former detainees who suffer collateral consequences as a result of their detention, the consequences identified by the petitioners did not constitute the kind of injuries sufficient to give the court jurisdiction. Although petitioners claimed that their designation as enemy combatants caused the countries to which they were transferred to restrict their travel, the *Gul* panel did not find this to be an injury redressible by the court, because the restrictions were imposed by the foreign governments rather than the United States. The panel also was not persuaded by petitioners' claim that they suffered a cognizable injury because their "enemy combatants" designation barred their travel to the United States. As an initial matter, the panel noted that there was no evidence that petitioners actually wanted to enter the United States. Moreover, the court ruled that even the plaintiffs' designation as enemy combatants was rescinded, this would not remove the barriers to U.S. travel; by statute, all Guantanamo detainees were placed on the government's "no fly" list, regardless of enemy combatant status, and U.S. immigration law's restrictions on the admission of aliens posing security risks was not dependent upon an enemy combatant designation. The panel also deemed petitioners' claim that their designation meant that they remained subject to possible targeting by the United States as "the most speculative [claim] of all," as the petitioners had "no basis whatsoever for believing" the government might still pursue them after releasing them from custody. Finally, the court found that binding precedent foreclosed consideration of petitioners' argument that they suffered a cognizable injury on the basis of the stigma caused by their designation.

The petitioners have sought to appeal the *Gul* decision to the Supreme Court, but the Court has yet to decide whether to review the case.

Other Notable Rulings

Besides the rulings discussed above, the appellate court for the D.C. Circuit has also issued opinions on several other distinct issues related to U.S. detention policy. These rulings have involved issues including, *inter alia*, the continuing application of the judicial review procedures established under DTA following the Supreme Court's ruling in *Boumediene v. Bush*; the ability of former Guantanamo detainees to bring civil suit against U.S. officials based on the detainees' allegedly wrongful treatment while in U.S. custody; and the application of the constitutional writ of habeas to persons held by the United States in foreign locations other than Guantanamo.

Parhat v. Gates, 532 F.3d 834 (D.C. Cir. 2008)

In June 2008, a three-judge panel of the D.C. Circuit ruled in the case of *Parhat v. Gates* that the petitioner had been improperly deemed an "enemy combatant" by a Combatant Status Review Tribunal (CSRT), the first ruling of its kind by a federal court. The ruling, which occurred prior to the Supreme Court's decision in *Boumediene*, was made under the judicial review process that had been established by the DTA. Although the D.C. Circuit has since held that the DTA review process is no longer in effect, the *Parhat* decision continues to be cited within the D.C. Circuit for its holding that evidence presented by the government must be in a form that permits a reviewing court to assess its reliability.[50]

---

[50] Indeed, the D.C. Circuit in *Bismullah* implied that, despite its determination that the DTA review process was no longer available to detainees, the circuit court's ruling in *Parhat* remained in force. *Bismullah*, 551 F.3d 1068, 1075, n. 2 (D.C. Cir. 2009). *See also* Bensayah v. Obama, 610 F.3d 718, 725-726 (D.C. Cir. 2010) ("In *Parhat* we made clear that the reliability of evidence can be determined not only by looking at the evidence alone but, alternatively, by considering 'sufficient additional information ... permit[ting the fact finder] to assess its reliability.'"); Ameziane v. (continued...)

The petitioner in *Parhat*, an ethnic Chinese Uighur captured in Pakistan in December 2001, was found by a CSRT to be subject to detention on account of his affiliation with a Uighur independence group known as the East Turkistan Islamic Movement (ETIM), which was purportedly "associated" with Al Qaeda and the Taliban and engaged in hostilities against the United States and its coalition partners (the petitioner denied membership in the ETIM). The *Parhat* panel found that the evidence presented by the government to support its claims regarding the ETIM was insufficient to support the CSRT's determination that Parhat was an enemy combatant. Most significantly, the court found that the principal evidence presented by the government regarding the ETIM being associated with Al Qaeda and the Taliban and engaged in hostilities against the United States and its coalition allies—four government intelligence documents describing ETIM activities and the group's relationship with Al Qaeda and the Taliban—did not "provide any of the underlying reporting upon which the documents' bottom-line assertions are founded, nor any assessment of the reliability of that reporting."[51] As a result, the Circuit Court found that neither the CSRT nor the reviewing court itself were capable of assessing the reliability of the assertions made by the documents. Accordingly "those bare assertions cannot sustain the determination that Parhat is an enemy combatant,"[52] and the CSRT's designation was therefore improper. The circuit court stressed that it was not suggesting that hearsay evidence could never reliably be used to determine whether a person was an enemy combatant, or that the government must always submit the basis for its factual assertions to enable an assessment of its claims. However, evidence "must be presented in a form, or with sufficient additional information, that permits the [CSRT] and court to assess its reliability."[53]

The *Parhat* panel also denied without prejudice a government motion to protect from public disclosure any nonclassified information raised in the litigation that the executive branch had labeled "law enforcement sensitive," along with names and identifying information of U.S. personnel mentioned in the record. While the panel acknowledged that information falling under both of these categories warranted protection from public disclosure, it characterized the government's argument for nondisclosure as being supported only upon "a generic explanation of the need for protection, providing no rationale specific to the information actually at issue in this case." In particular, the panel faulted the government motion for failing either to "give the court a basis for withholding" a specific category of information, or a basis upon which the court could "determine whether the information it has designated properly falls within the categories it has described."

Bismullah v. Gates, 551 F.3d 1068 (D.C. Cir. 2009)[54]

This case concerned the continuing availability of DTA review procedures in light of the Supreme Court's ruling in *Boumediene v. Bush* that the constitutional privilege of habeas corpus extends to non-citizen detainees held at Guantanamo. As discussed *supra*, following the Supreme Court's ruling in *Gates v. Bismullah*, the D.C. Circuit reinstated two earlier rulings concerning the scope

---

(...continued)
Obama, 620 F.3d 1 (D.C. Cir. 2010) (holding that district court had failed to properly apply *Parhat* in its consideration of government motion to designate certain information as "protected" under the governing protective order).

[51] Parhat v. Gates, 532 F.3d 834, 846-47 (D.C. Cir. 2008).

[52] *Id.* at 847.

[53] *Id.* at 849.

[54] A more detailed discussion of the *Bismullah* case is found in CRS Report RL33180, *Enemy Combatant Detainees: Habeas Corpus Challenges in Federal Court*, by Jennifer K. Elsea and Michael John Garcia.

of judicial review of CSRT determinations available under the DTA. The government subsequently petitioned for a rehearing of the case, arguing that the Supreme Court's ruling in *Boumediene* effectively nullified the review system established by the DTA, as Congress had not intended for detainees to have two judicial forums in which to challenge their detention. The D.C. Circuit granted the government's motion for rehearing, and in *Bismullah v. Gates*, a three-judge panel held that, in light of the Supreme Court's ruling in *Boumediene* restoring detainees' ability to seek habeas review of the legality of their detention, the appellate court no longer had jurisdiction over petitions for review filed pursuant to the DTA.

Rasul v. Myers, 563 F.3d 527 (D.C. Cir. 2009) *(per curiam)*, *cert. denied*, 130 S.Ct. 1013 (2009)

Four British nationals formerly detained at Guantanamo sued the Secretary of Defense and various military officers for damages, alleging that their treatment while in U.S. military custody violated their rights under the Fifth and Eighth Amendments to the Constitution, the Geneva Conventions, and other provisions of law. The district court dismissed the *Bivens*[55] claims on the basis of qualified immunity, holding that the officers could not reasonably be expected to have anticipated that the plaintiffs, as aliens held overseas, would be entitled to rights under the U.S. Constitution.[56] The D.C. Circuit twice affirmed,[57] interpreting *Boumediene* (on remand) as "disclaim[ing] any intention to disturb existing law governing the extraterritorial reach of any constitutional provisions, other than the Suspension Clause,"[58] which, in the circuit court's view, appears to mean that those detained at Guantanamo have no rights under the Constitution (other than the right to petition for habeas corpus). It rested its holding, however, on its analysis of qualified immunity under *Bivens*, agreeing with the lower court that even if the Constitution does provide some protections to the plaintiffs, the defendants were protected by qualified immunity. Even were this not so clear, the D.C. Circuit noted a "special factor" precludes extending a *Bivens* remedy to plaintiffs; namely, the "[t]he danger of obstructing U.S. national security policy."[59]

Having found that the claims for damages were barred by the Federal Tort Claims Act, the circuit court did not address whether *Boumediene*'s holding invalidating Section 7 of the MCA encompassed only the portion of the provision that stripped courts of jurisdiction over habeas claims, or whether the language eliminating other causes of action against the government had also been invalidated.[60] Subsequently in *Al-Zahrani v. Rodriguez*, discussed *infra*, the D.C.

---

[55] Bivens v. Six Unknown Agents of Fed. Bureau of Narcotics, 403 U.S. 388 (1971) (providing for cause of action in tort for violation of certain constitutional rights).

[56] Rasul v. Rumsfeld, 414 F. Supp. 2d 26 (D.D.C. 2006).

[57] Rasul v. Myers, 512 F.3d 644 (D.C. Cir. 2008) ("Rasul I") was vacated by the Supreme court and remanded for reconsideration in light of *Boumediene*. 129 S.Ct. 763 (2008) Rasul v. Myers, 563 F.3d 527 (D.C. Cir. 2009) ("Rasul II") reinstated the earlier opinion but limited its scope to rest the holding on qualified immunity without adjudicating the constitutional questions. The appellate court reversed a holding by the district court that would have enabled plaintiffs to pursue claims based on the Religious Freedom Restoration Act (RFRA), 42 U.S.C. §§2000bb *et seq*.

[58] *Rasul II*, 563 F.3d at 529.

[59] *Id*. at 532 & n.5.

[60] 28 U.S.C. §2241(e)(2), provides that "[n]o court ... shall have jurisdiction to hear or consider any other action against the United States or its agents relating to any aspect of the detention, transfer, treatment, trial, or conditions of confinement of an alien who is or was detained by the United States and has been determined by the United States to have been properly detained as an enemy combatant or is awaiting such determination."

Circuit held that the language in the MCA eliminating causes of action other than habeas corpus survived *Boumediene*.[61]

Maqaleh v. Gates, 605 F.3d 84 (D.C. Cir. 2010)

This case concerned the application of the constitutional writ of habeas corpus to non-citizens detained by the United States in Afghanistan. In 2009, a federal district court ruled that constitutional writ of habeas may extend to non-Afghan detainees held in a U.S.-operated facility in Bagram, Afghanistan, when those detainees had been captured outside of Afghanistan but were transferred to Bagram for long-term detention as enemy combatants. The district court held that the circumstances surrounding the detention of the petitioners in *Maqaleh* were "virtually identical to the detainees in *Boumediene*—they are [non-U.S.] citizens who were ... apprehended in foreign lands far from the United States and brought to yet another country for detention."[62]

A three-judge panel of the D.C. Circuit Court of Appeals reversed, and held that the constitutional writ of habeas did not extend to non-citizens detained in the Afghan theater of war. In making this determination, the circuit court applied factors listed by the Supreme Court in *Boumediene* as being relevant to analysis of the writ's extraterritorial application, namely, (1) the citizenship and status of the detainee and the adequacy of the status determination process; (2) the nature of the site where the person is seized and detained; and (3) practical obstacles inherent in resolving the prisoner's entitlement to the writ. According to the circuit panel, consideration of the first factor weighed in favor of extending the writ of habeas to the petitioners, because the status determination process employed in Afghanistan to determine whether persons were subject to detention afforded fewer procedural protections than the process used at Guantanamo.[63] However, the circuit panel found that the application of the other two enumerated factors conclusively weighed against extending the constitutional writ of habeas to non-citizens held at Bagram. In particular, the circuit panel found that the degree and likely duration of U.S. control over Bagram were more limited than U.S. control over Guantanamo. The panel also found that significant practical obstacles would be inherent in attempting to resolve the habeas claims of Bagram detainees, including the petitioners' location in an active theater of war. The court considered it pertinent that the Unites States held persons at Bagram pursuant to a cooperative agreement with the Afghan government, and suggested that extending constitutional protections to Bagram detainees could be disruptive to the U.S.-Afghan relationship.

---

[61] Prior to this decision, district court judges appeared to have uniformly agreed that *Boumediene* only invalidated the provision of the MCA stripping federal courts of habeas jurisdiction over Guantanamo detainees. *See, e.g.,* Khadr v. Bush, 587 F. Supp. 2d 225, 235-36 (D.D.C. 2009); *In re* Guantanamo Bay Detainee Litig., 577 F. Supp. 2d 312, 314 (D.D.C. 2008); *In re* Guantanamo Bay Detainee Litig., 570 F. Supp. 2d 13, 18 (D.D.C. 2008)). *See also* Kiyemba v. Obama, 561 F.3d 509, 512 n.1 (D.C. Cir. 2009) (in habeas case, noting that *Boumediene* "referred to §7 without specifying a particular subsection of §2241(e) but its discussion of the Suspension Clause clearly indicates it was referring only to that part of §7 codified at §2241(e)(1)")).

[62] Maqaleh v. Gates, 604 F. Supp. 2d 205 (D.D.C. 2009).

[63] After the district court's initial ruling in *Maqaleh*, the DOD announced modifications to the administrative process used to review the status of aliens held at Bagram, which would afford detainees greater procedural rights. The modified process does not contemplate judicial review of administrative determinations regarding the detention of persons at Bagram. *See* Letter from Phillip Carter, Dep. Asst. Sec. Defense for Detainee Policy, to Sen. Carl Levin, Chairman of Sen. Armed Serv. Comm., July 14, 2009, available at http://www.scotusblog.com/wp/wp-content/uploads/2009/09/US-Bagram-brief-9-14-09.pdf. The circuit panel stated that its analysis was not informed by these new procedures, as those procedures were not in place when the case was appealed to the circuit court.

Although the *Maqaleh* panel held that the constitutional writ of habeas did not extend to persons in petitioners' situation, it suggested that its analysis might be different if evidence were presented that the executive branch opted to transfer detainees into a theater of war to evade judicial review. Relying on this statement, the *Maqaleh* petitioners sought a rehearing of their habeas claims. In February 2011, a lower district court permitted the petitioners to amend their habeas complaint to take into account new evidence that purportedly undercut the reasoning of the *Maqaleh* panel. Litigation in the case is ongoing.

Al-Zahrani v. Rodriguez, 669 F.3d 315 (D.C. Cir. 2012)

In *Al-Zahrani*, a three-judge panel of the D.C. Circuit upheld the dismissal of a civil suit brought against federal officials by the fathers of two foreign nationals who had been detained as "enemy combatants" at Guantanamo and died in U.S. custody. The circuit panel held that dismissal was warranted under Section 7(a)(2) of the MCA, which stripped federal courts of jurisdiction over non-habeas claims brought against the government concerning the detention of aliens designated as "enemy combatants." While the Supreme Court in *Boumediene* had struck down the MCA's bar on federal court jurisdiction over habeas claims, the *Al-Zahrani* panel recognized that the MCA's separate jurisdictional bar over non-habeas claims remained in effect. Although plaintiffs' contented that Section 7(a)(2) was unconstitutional because it denied plaintiffs "a proper remedy for violations of their constitutional rights." The panel rejected this claim because the only remedy that plaintiffs sought was money damages, and "such remedies are not constitutionally required" and may be barred by statutory or common law immunities.

Rulings by the Fourth Circuit Court of Appeals

Although most judicial activity concerning U.S. detention policy has occurred in the D.C. Circuit, a few notable cases have been decided in the Fourth Circuit Court of Appeals. Each case concerned the military detention of a U.S. person within the United States—one a U.S. citizen and the other an alien lawfully admitted into the country on a student visa—following the Executive's determination that the person was an unlawful enemy combatant. In each case, the individual was ultimately transferred to civilian custody, and thereafter tried and convicted for terrorism-related activity. Nonetheless, it is possible that the circuit court's analysis of the scope of executive detention authority may inform subsequent judicial rulings on the matter.

Padilla v. Hanft, 423 F.3d 386 (4th Cir. 2005)

After the Supreme Court vacated an earlier ruling in his favor by the Second Circuit (see above), Jose Padilla filed a new petition in the District Court for the District of South Carolina. The district court granted Padilla's motion for summary judgment and ordered the government to release him from military detention, while suggesting Padilla could be kept in civilian custody if charged with a crime or determined to be a material witness.[64] Padilla's attorneys had based their argument on the dissenting opinion of four Supreme Court Justices, who would have found Padilla's detention barred by the Non-Detention Act, 18 U.S.C. §4001(a), and the language in *Hamdi* seemingly limiting the scope of detention authority under the AUMF to combatants

---

[64] Padilla v. Hanft, 389 F. Supp. 2d 678 (D.S.C. 2005).

captured in Afghanistan. The government argued that Padilla's detention was covered under the *Hamdi* decision's interpretation of the AUMF as an act of Congress authorizing his detention because he is alleged to have attended an Al Qaeda training camp in Afghanistan before traveling to Pakistan and then to the United States.[65] The judge disagreed with the government, finding that more express authority from Congress would be necessary and that the AUMF contains no such authority. Accordingly, the court found Padilla's detention barred by 18 U.S.C. §4001(a). The court also disagreed that the President has inherent authority as Commander-in-Chief of the Armed Forces to determine wartime measures.[66]

The Fourth Circuit Court of Appeals reversed, finding that Padilla, although captured in the United States, could be detained pursuant to the AUMF because he had been, prior to returning to the United States, "'armed and present in a combat zone' in Afghanistan as part of Taliban forces during the conflict there with the United States."[67] As the Supreme Court again considered whether to grant review, the government charged Padilla with conspiracy based on evidence unrelated to the original "dirty bomb" plot allegations and petitioned for leave to transfer him from military custody to a federal prison for civilian trial.[68] The Court granted the government permission to transfer Padilla[69] and later denied certiorari.[70] Padilla was found guilty and sentenced to 17 years and three months' imprisonment, the trial court having rejected his motion to dismiss charges against him due to his alleged mistreatment at the hands of the military.[71]

---

[65] *See* Respondents' Answer to the Petition for a Writ of Habeas Corpus at 2, Padilla v. Hanft, C/A No. 02:04 2221-26AJ (D.S.C. filed 2004).

[66] 389 F. Supp. 2d at 690.

[67] 423 F.3d 386, 390-91 (4th Cir. 2005).

[68] The government initially asked the Fourth Circuit to approve Padilla's transfer and suggested it should vacate its opinion, but the judges preferred to defer to the Supreme Court to make that determination. In rejecting the government's application, Circuit Judge Luttig (who has since stepped down from the bench) issued a harsh opinion expressing disappointment at the government's decision abruptly to abandon its position that national security imperatives demanded Padilla's continued military detention:

> [A]s the government surely must understand, although the various facts it has asserted are not necessarily inconsistent or without basis, its actions have left not only the impression that Padilla may have been held for these years, even if justifiably, by mistake—an impression we would have thought the government could ill afford to leave extant. They have left the impression that the government may even have come to the belief that the principle in reliance upon which it has detained Padilla for this time, that the President possesses the authority to detain enemy combatants who enter into this country for the purpose of attacking America and its citizens from within, can, in the end, yield to expediency with little or no cost to its conduct of the war against terror—an impression we would have thought the government likewise could ill afford to leave extant.

Padilla v. Hanft, 432 F.3d 582, 587 (4th Cir. 2005)(order).

[69] Padilla v. Hanft, 546 U.S. 1084 (2006).

[70] 547 U.S. 1062 (2006).

[71] United States v. Padilla, 2007 WL 1079090 (S.D.Fla. 2007) (unreported opinion). While one district court held Padilla can pursue civil damages against a former government official for his treatment in military detention, Padilla v. Yoo, 633 F. Supp. 2d 1005 (N.D.Cal. 2009), the Fourth Circuit has rejected a civil suit on the basis of qualified immunity for the government officials involved, Lebron v. Rumsfeld, 670 F.3d 540 (4th Cir. 2012)

al-Marri v. Pucciarelli, 534 F.3d 213 (4th Cir. 2008) *(per curiam)*[72]

In *al-Marri*, the Fourth Circuit sitting *en banc* considered whether the AUMF and the law of war permit the detention of a resident alien alleged to have engaged in activities within the United States in support of Al Qaeda, but who had not been part of the conflict in Afghanistan. Four of the nine judges would have held that even if the allegations were true, al-Marri did not fit within the legal category of "enemy combatant" within the meaning of *Hamdi*, and that the government could continue to hold him only if it charged him with a crime, commenced deportation proceedings, or obtained a material witness warrant in connection with grand jury proceedings (as a majority of the original three-judge panel had found). A plurality of the fractured *en banc* court, however, found that the AUMF and the law of war give the President the power to detain persons who enter the United States as "sleeper agents" on behalf of Al Qaeda for the purpose of committing hostile and war-like acts such as those carried out on 9/11 (although the judges did not arrive at a common definition of "enemy combatant"). The case was remanded to the district court for further consideration of the evidence to determine whether the government had established that al-Marri was a sleeper agent.

The *en banc* panel also considered the evidentiary burden that the government would be required to fulfill to detain al-Marri as an enemy combatant. In his controlling opinion, Judge Traxler wrote that the lower court had erred in applying the relaxed evidentiary standards of *Hamdi* to persons captured in the United States. While the *Hamdi* plurality suggested that hearsay evidence might be sufficient to support detention of a person apprehended in combat zone, Judge Traxler wrote that *Hamdi* does not establish a "cookie-cutter procedure appropriate for every alleged enemy-combatant, regardless of the circumstances of the alleged combatant's seizure or the actual burdens the government might face in defending the *habeas* petition in the normal way."[73] However, he recognized that some relaxation of normal procedural safeguards may be warranted if the government demonstrates the need for this relaxation on account of national security interests and an undue burden that would result if it was compelled to produce more reliable evidence.

After the Supreme Court granted review, the government brought charges against al-Marri in federal court and asked the Court to dismiss the case as moot and to vacate the decision below, which the Court agreed to do, leaving the applicability of the AUMF to persons captured in the United States uncertain. Al-Marri pled guilty to conspiring to provide material support to terrorists and was sentenced to eight and a half years in prison.

Lebron v. Rumsfeld, 670 F.3d 540 (4th Cir. 2012)

This 2012 decision concerned a civil suit brought by Jose Padilla and his mother against current and former government officials based on Padilla's prior military detention as an enemy combatant (Padilla's habeas challenge to military detention is discussed *supra*). The petitioners sought a declaration that Padilla's detention was unconstitutional, an order enjoining any future

---

[72] For further discussion of *al-Marri*, see CRS Report RL33180, *Enemy Combatant Detainees: Habeas Corpus Challenges in Federal Court*, by Jennifer K. Elsea and Michael John Garcia; CRS Report R42337, *Detention of U.S. Persons as Enemy Belligerents*, by Jennifer K. Elsea.

[73] al-Marri v. Pucciarelli, 534 F.3d 213, 221 (2008) (Traxler, J., concurring).

designation as an enemy combatant, and nominal damages. The district court dismissed the suit, and a three-judge circuit panel affirmed.

The panel construed all but one of petitioners' claims to ask the judiciary to imply a cause of action for constitutional violations by federal officials (i.e., a *Bivens* claim). The panel stated that special factors "counsel judicial hesitation in implying causes of action for enemy combatants held in military detention."[74] The Constitution designates the political branches with authority over military affairs, with no comparable role accorded to the judiciary. According to the panel, judicial involvement in such matters would "stray from the traditional subjects of judicial competence,"[75] and risk impingement upon the explicit constitutional responsibilities of the political branches. The panel also characterized the judiciary as ill-equipped to administer a *Bivens* remedy the case before it, as litigation would risk interrupting the military chain of command by requiring members of the Armed Forces and their civilian superiors to testify about each other's decisions and actions, and could also interfere with military and intelligence operations on a wide scale. Finally, the panel found that Padilla had "extensive opportunities to challenge the legal basis for his detention"[76] in prior habeas litigation, and the existence of alternative avenues for protecting his interests counseled against recognition of a *Bivens* action.

In addition to his *Bivens* claims, Padilla also brought action under the Religious Freedom Restoration Act (RFRA) for alleged burdens to his free exercise of religion that were caused by his military detention. While not going so far as to absolutely rule that RFRA did not apply to persons held in military detention, the panel found that there were "strong reasons for defendants to believe that RFRA did not apply to enemy combatants," and it was appropriate to recognize an immunity defense in the present situation because "it would run counter to basic notions of notice and fair warning to hold that personal liability in such an unsettled area of law might attach."[77]

The panel also upheld the lower court's ruling that Padilla lacked standing to seek an order enjoining the government from designating him as an enemy combatant in the future. The panel held that the lower court had properly found that Padilla suffered no real and immediate risk of harm from this designation, as he was in the process of serving a long-term prison sentence due to his criminal conviction for terrorist activities. Any additional reputational harm that Padilla suffered on account of his designation as an enemy combatant was also deemed to be inadequate to provide Padilla with standing.

Criminal Cases

Although numerous cases have been brought in federal civilian court involving persons who allegedly engaged in terrorist activity, relatively few involve persons who were captured abroad by U.S. forces during operations against either Al Qaeda or the Taliban, and only one case has been tried in civilian court involving a person involved in the September 11, 2001, terrorist attacks. This section discusses notable rulings made in criminal cases involving Zacharias Moussaoui, who was tried and convicted for his role in the September 11, 2001, terrorist attacks, but was never officially designated as an "enemy combatant"; John Walker Lindh, thus far the

---

[74] Lebron v. Rumsfeld, 670 F.3d 540, 548 (4th Cir. 2012).
[75] *Id.*
[76] *Id.* at 556.
[77] *Id.* at 557.

only person captured abroad and tried and convicted in federal civilian court for belligerent activities occurring on the Afghan battlefield; and Ahmed Khalfan Ghailani, a suspect in the 1998 African Embassy bombings who was incarcerated at Guantanamo and charged at a military commission, but was later transferred to the Southern District of New York for trial on terrorism charges. Ghailani is the only Guantanamo prisoner to have been transferred for civilian trial in the United States.

Moussaoui Litigation

Zacharias Moussaoui, a French citizen, was arrested by immigration authorities for overstaying his visa after he raised suspicions at a Minnesota flight school where he was enrolled. Less than a month after he was taken into custody, a group of Al Qaeda terrorists carried out the September 11, 2001, attacks, and Moussaoui was charged in connection with the conspiracy to commit those attacks. On January 7, 2002, after Moussaoui's arraignment, the Department of Justice (DOJ) imposed Special Administrative Measures (SAMs) to prevent his communication with other terrorists. Moussaoui was permitted unmonitored attorney/client and consular communications and mail, and monitored communications with others. The court also issued a protective order under the Classified Information Procedures Act (CIPA; 18 U.S.C. app. 3, §3), which permitted defense counsel to access classified information, but did not permit Moussaoui to receive such information unless the government consented or the judge determined that it was necessary to protect his right to prepare a defense.

After a competency hearing in which the judge explained that the lack of personal access to classified information could impede Moussaoui's ability to defend himself without counsel appropriately cleared for access to such information, the judge permitted the defendant to proceed *pro se*, and appointed the public defenders who had been assigned to the case to act as standby counsel. After Moussaoui refused to cooperate with his appointed lawyers, the judge replaced some of them, but ultimately concluded that Moussaoui was unlikely to approve any court-appointed attorneys, and also held that he was not entitled to unmonitored access to "advisory counsel" of his choice. Despite Moussaoui's rejection of virtually all efforts by standby counsel to assist him, the lawyers continued to file motions on his behalf, including motions seeking relief from the SAMs or to revoke his *pro se* status on the grounds that he was not in a position to take advantage of exculpatory information in the government's possession. Moussaoui attempted to plead guilty in July 2002, but was unwilling to admit to the facts necessary to support the plea and withdrew it.

Moussaoui then sought access to several persons held overseas by the government as enemy combatants who might provide information that would be useful to his defense by testifying that Moussaoui was not involved in the September 11 attacks. (The government had advanced theories that Moussaoui was the intended "20th hijacker" or pilot of a fifth plane intended to target the White House, whose participation in the actual attack was thwarted due to his incarceration, and that Moussaoui's refusal to provide agents information about the plot that might have prevented the attacks from taking place contributed to the deaths of the several thousand victims, a factor relevant to death penalty eligibility. Moussaoui claimed to be part of a plan for subsequent terrorist operations and to have had no knowledge regarding the September 11 plot.) The government offered to provide redacted summaries of reports presumably based on intelligence interrogations of the enemy combatant witnesses,[78] but the judge rejected the

---

[78] The exact nature of the information and its acquisition by the government is obscured by the many redactions in the (continued...)

proffered substitutions as possibly unreliable and inadequate to protect Moussaoui's Sixth Amendment right to compulsory process.

The government appealed the district court's order requiring the government to make three of the requested enemy combatant witnesses available for deposition to be conducted by remote video. The United States Court of Appeals for the Fourth Circuit affirmed the district court's holding that that the enemy combatants in question could be reached through judicial process (directed at their custodians) for the purpose of providing testimony and that their testimony would be relevant to the case, but reversed the order for depositions and the sanctions the court had imposed for the government's refusal to comply.[79] The appellate court held that substitutions for depositions could be prepared that would provide substantially the same ability to prepare a defense, although it agreed with some of the objections the district court had articulated regarding the government's proposed substitutions. The majority viewed the intelligence reports as possessing adequate indicia of reliability because they were produced through methods designed to produce accurate analyses of foreign intelligence.[80] Consequently, the court remanded the case to the district court with instructions to prepare substitutions for the deposition testimony by a process involving collaboration with the parties,[81] noting that adequate jury instructions would be necessary in some cases to permit the jury to assess the reliability of the evidence.

In the meantime, the district court revoked Moussaoui's *pro se* privilege for his continued submission of improper filings, some of which contained veiled or overt threats, political statements with no relevance to the case, attempts at communicating to persons overseas, and insulting language, despite repeated warnings that such conduct would result in sanctions. After the Supreme Court denied certiorari with respect to the appellate court's ruling on his right to depose enemy combatant witnesses in the custody of the United States, Moussaoui again decided, over his counsel's objections, to plead guilty as an apparent tactic to avoid the death penalty. After a hearing in which Moussaoui demonstrated to the court's satisfaction that he understood a guilty plea would result in forfeiting his right to appeal based on any violation of his constitutional

---

(...continued)
reported opinions.

[79] United States v. Moussaoui, 382 F.3d 453, 456-57 (4th Cir. 2004) ("*Moussaoui II*"). In "*Moussaoui I*," 333 F.3d 509, 517 (4th Cir. 2003), the circuit court dismissed the appeal of the discovery order as unripe and remanded for the government to propose substitutions for the witness testimony similar to those available under CIPA. (CIPA applies to the production of documents during discovery but does not address witnesses). The district court imposed sanctions on remand after the government refused to make the enemy combatant witnesses available for deposition. The judge rejected the parties' proposal for an order of dismissal, the ordinary sanction under CIPA in cases in which the government declines to provide classified information the court has determined is necessary for the defense. Instead, she dismissed the death notice on the grounds that the witnesses could provide testimony that might preclude a jury from finding Moussaoui eligible for the death penalty. Because the testimony could exonerate Moussaoui of involvement in the September 11 attacks, the district court prohibited the government "from making any argument, or offering any evidence, suggesting that the defendant had any involvement in, or knowledge of, the September 11 attacks." United States v. Moussaoui, 282 F. Supp. 2d 480, 327 (E.D. Va. 2003). Evidence that would have been excluded under the order included cockpit voice recordings, video footage showing the collapse of the World Trade Center Towers, and photographs of victims.

[80] 382 F.3d at 487 n. 31. Judge Gregory noted in dissent that such information may be reliable for intelligence purposes and yet omit relevant information that might be helpful to the defense because such information was not deemed to have any actionable foreign intelligence value. *Id.* at 488, n. 6.

[81] As noted by a dissenting judge of the appellate panel, the procedures crafted by the majority deviate from CIPA procedures by having the district judge, rather than the government, prepare the substitutions for the potential testimony, arguably making the district court judge an advocate in the proceedings. 382 F.3d. at 484-85 (Gregory, J., concurring in part and dissenting in part).

rights that might have occurred prior to the plea, the court accepted his plea. Moussaoui admitted to the government's allegations, including some he had previously denied, and signed the statement of facts supporting the guilty plea, adding the designation of "20th Hijacker" below his signature. During the sentencing phase, Moussaoui claimed that his mission on September 11 was to have been piloting a commercial airliner into the White House, although statements by enemy combatant witnesses introduced by the government contradicted that claim, along with some other allegations Moussaoui had admitted as true. In the bifurcated sentencing proceeding, the jury found Moussaoui to be eligible to receive the death penalty but declined to impose it, sentencing him instead to life in prison.

Just days after receiving his sentence, Moussaoui filed a motion to withdraw his guilty plea, claiming that his understanding of the American legal system had been "completely flawed" and asking for a new trial "[b]ecause I now see that it is possible that I can receive a fair trial ... even with Americans as jurors and that I can have the opportunity to prove that I did not have any knowledge of and was not a member of the plot to hijack planes and crash them into buildings on September 11, 2001."[82] He then appealed the court's denial of his motion for a new trial, arguing among other things that his plea was not voluntary as a matter of law because of district court rulings that violated his constitutional rights, and that it was not knowing because he did not have access to classified information in the government's possession that contradicted the government's theory of the case. Finding that his guilty plea was entered with full knowledge and understanding of its ramifications and that his objections to constitutional claims were waived, the circuit court affirmed. The circuit court reviewed the procedural history regarding Moussaoui's access to classified information because these claims were relevant to the adequacy of the plea and were therefore not waived for purposes of appeal, but reiterated its earlier view that adequate substitutions under CIPA would have protected Moussaoui's rights had the CIPA process not been cut short by the guilty plea. Moreover, it noted that CIPA information had been made available during the sentencing phase for establishing death-eligibility factors, and that not only did Moussaoui make no effort to withdraw his plea upon receiving the information, but he contradicted the supposedly exculpatory statements at trial. Finally, the circuit court rejected Moussaoui's contention that plain error had resulted in the jury's false belief that the only sentencing options available to them were the death penalty or life imprisonment without possibility of parole, in violation of his right to have his sentence decided by the jury, on the basis that Moussaoui had requested the jury be instructed that the sentencing options were limited as part of an apparently successful strategy to avoid the death penalty.

United States v. Lindh, 227 F. Supp. 2d 565 (E.D. Va. 2004)

John Walker Lindh, a U.S. citizen, was captured in Afghanistan and charged with 10 counts of supplying services to the Taliban under various statutes. He moved to have the charges dismissed, arguing, *inter alia* that he was entitled to combatant immunity as part of the Taliban. While the judge refused to accept the government's argument that the President's designation of Lindh as an "unlawful combatant" was not subject to second-guessing by the court, he nevertheless concluded that the Taliban is not entitled to combatant immunity under international law and rejected the defense.[83]

---

[82] Moussaoui v. Obama, 591 F.3d 263, 278 (4th Cir. 2010).

[83] United States v. Lindh, 212 F. Supp. 2d 541, 557-58 (E.D. Va. 2002). The judge also rejected Lindh's contention that media publicity had rendered a fair trial for him impossible, at least in that particular court, and that the International (continued...)

Lindh was also unsuccessful in his bid to avoid the government's request for a protective order covering unclassified but sensitive information as well as classified information that the government had concluded was subject to discovery by the defendant.[84] At issue was whether the defendant could adequately prepare a defense given the government's proposal to restrict certain information from the government's redacted reports of relevant interviews with detainees held at Guantanamo. Rule 16(d) of the Federal Rules for Criminal Procedure permits the court to restrict discovery with respect to any information for good cause, including cases where the government claims the protection of such information is vital to the national security. The court found good cause to issue a protective order to prohibit the public dissemination of the detainee interview reports, which would serve to prevent Al Qaeda members from learning "the status of, the methods used in, and the information obtained from the ongoing investigation of the detainees."[85] Lindh objected to the order on the basis that it would burden his ability to prepare for trial by requiring the pre-screening of investigators and expert witnesses before he would be permitted to disclose unclassified information to them, which he argued could reveal his defense strategy to the prosecution. The judge found the needs of both parties could be accommodated by amending the proposed order to require investigators or expert witnesses for the defense to sign a memorandum of understanding, under oath, promising not to disclose information provided under the order, rather than requiring pre-screening. Lindh also objected to the proposed protective order because he believed it would impair his ability to use the media to influence public opinion, as he contended the government had done. Noting that the "[d]efendant has no constitutional right to use the media to influence public opinion concerning his case so as to gain an advantage at trial" under either the Sixth Amendment right to a public trial or the public's First Amendment right to a free press,[86] the judge rejected the argument, but cautioned that information that turned out to be relevant and material to the trial as the case progressed might eventually require unsealing to further those rights.[87]

Prior to the beginning of the merits phase of the trial, Lindh struck a plea deal with prosecutors, admitting to one count of carrying an explosive during the commission of a felony, and was sentenced to 20 years' imprisonment.

United States v. Ghailani, No. S10 98 Crim. 1023 (S.D.N.Y.)

Alleged Al Qaeda member Ahmed Khalfan Ghailani was indicted in 1998 and charged with conspiracy to kill Americans abroad in connection with the bombing the United States Embassies in Nairobi, Kenya, and Dar es Salaam, Tanzania. He was arrested in Pakistan in 2004 and turned over to U.S. custody to be held and interrogated at an undisclosed site abroad by Central Intelligence Agency (CIA) officials. In 2006, he was transferred to DOD custody and held as an enemy combatant at Guantanamo. He was charged before a military commission for his role in one of the embassy bombings, but the charges were later withdrawn so that he could be transferred to the Southern District of New York to be tried on the earlier indictment. The transfer

---

(...continued)

Economic Emergency Powers Act ("IEEPA") (50 U.S.C. §1701 *et seq.*) regulations he was charged with violating were not valid.

[84] United States v. Lindh, 198 F. Supp. 2d 739 (E.D. Va. 2002).

[85] *Id.* at 742.

[86] *Id.* at 743.

[87] *Id.* at 744.

occurred in May 2009. Ghailani has since been convicted and sentenced to life imprisonment for his part in the conspiracy.

The case has resulted in a number of rulings on constitutional issues that are likely to be pertinent to the debate as to whether to try similar crimes in federal court or before military commissions, including such issues as the right to effective assistance of counsel, the right to a speedy trial, the privilege against self-incrimination and the right to counsel in custodial interrogation, and the consequences of a jury trial. How these issues might be resolved in a military commission or by reviewing courts remains to be seen. A military commission would also have had to resolve the issue of whether crimes committed prior to the 9/11 attacks can properly be charged as war crimes, a highly charged question for which arguments can be made either way, but which appears to be lacking in precedent.

After his transfer to New York, Ghailani moved for an injunction or other relief against the Secretary of Defense to prevent the reassignment of the military defense attorneys who had been detailed to serve as his defense counsel before the military commission. Ghailani urged the court to order the government to permit the two officers to act as his appointed counsel in federal court, arguing that depriving him of the assistance of the counsel he had grown to trust amounted to a violation of his Sixth Amendment right to the effective assistance of counsel. The government urged the court to decline to adjudicate the motion or grant relief based on the political question doctrine, arguing that the assignment of military officers to particular duties is the prerogative of the executive branch alone. The judge did not think the political question doctrine prevented his consideration of the matter, since he was not considering the propriety of the reassignment as much as he was assessing the impact of the decision on the defendant's rights, but ultimately denied the motion, holding that an indigent defendant's right to appointed representation does not mean the right to continuous representation by counsel of his choice.[88]

Ghailani also filed a motion for dismissal of his indictment based on his claim that the government violated his Sixth Amendment right to a speedy trial. In connection with this motion, Ghailani sought discovery of documents in the government's possession that demonstrate the government delayed his prosecution from 2004 until his transfer to New York for reasons other than national security. Rule 16 of the Federal Rules for Criminal Procedure permits discovery of items "within the government's custody, possession, or control" that are material to the case, excluding documents that were prepared by government attorneys or agents that constitute work product connected to the prosecution. The judge excluded one document specifically requested by the defendant as attorney work product, but approved a more general request for information relating to the reasons behind the timing of Ghailani's transfer for trial based on a Supreme Court ruling that makes the "reason for delay" one part of the test for determining whether charges must be dismissed for failure to provide a speedy trial.[89] The judge defined the scope of "in the government's possession, custody, or control" as reaching beyond the officials of the U.S. Attorney's Office who had worked on the case to include higher-level DOJ officials who were not intimately involved in the case but were involved in the decision about where to prosecute Ghailani. This requirement will not unduly burden the prosecution with unreasonable discovery requirements, according to the court, because the embassy bombing crime had "commanded the attention of the highest levels" of the government long before Ghailani was in American custody.

---

[88] United States v. Ghailani, 686 F. Supp. 2d 279, 298-99 (S.D.N.Y 2009) (citing Morris v. Slappy, 461 U.S. 1, 14 (1983); Wheat v. United States, 486 U.S. 153, 159 (1988)).

[89] United States v. Ghailani, 687 F. Supp. 2d 365, 369 (S.D.N.Y. 2010) (citing Barker v. Wingo, 407 U.S. 514 (1972)).

Under these circumstances, high-level officials involved in the important decisions involving Ghailani's treatment can be included within the meaning of "government" in Rule 16.[90] Accordingly, the judge issued an order requiring production of documents held by the DOJ that are material to the case and not otherwise privileged under the rule.

The court ultimately denied the speedy trial motion after applying the multi-factor balancing test established by the Supreme Court in *Barker v. Wingo*,[91] which takes into account the length of the delay, the reason for the delay, the defendant's assertion of the right, and the prejudice to the defendant.[92] The court held that the time Ghailani spent in CIA detention was justified by the need to interrogate him for intelligence purposes, a process that was incompatible with prosecution in federal court.[93] The time between Ghailani's transfer to Guantanamo in 2006 and his transfer to New York in 2009, however, was held insufficient to justify postponement of trial, because the need to prevent the defendant from returning to hostilities was not incompatible with federal prosecution.[94] The aborted military commission prosecution did not justify delay because the government had complete discretion as to where to prosecute the defendant.[95] However, although the Guantanamo portion of the delay was attributable to the government, it was assessed as a "neutral factor" because there was no evidence that its purpose had to do with a "quest for tactical advantage."[96] Because Ghailani was detainable as an "enemy combatant" with or without prosecution, the need to avoid excessive incarceration was not a relevant factor under *Barker* analysis, either. The court was not persuaded that Ghailani was prejudiced by the delay, and it held there was no violation of his Sixth Amendment rights.

Although Ghailani's overseas detention by the CIA did not preclude his prosecution, it did result in the exclusion of a government witness whose identity was uncovered during Ghailani's interrogation and whose cooperation with prosecutors was less than willing.[97] The government having stipulated that any statements Ghailani made to CIA interrogators were coerced, the judge held that the Fifth Amendment's privilege against self-incrimination would permit the government to introduce such witness testimony only if it had proven that the connection between Ghailani's coerced statements and the witness's testimony was sufficiently remote or attenuated to purge the taint of illegality, or if it could establish another basis upon which the testimony could be admitted. The government failed to establish the inevitability of its identification of the witness independent of the defendant's coerced statement, and it did not persuade the judge that the "core application" doctrine applicable to the exclusionary rule in the Fourth Amendment

---

[90] *Id.* at 372.

[91] Barker v. Wingo, Warden 407 U.S. 514, 519 (1972).

[92] *See id.* at 530. Courts have recognized at least three types of prejudice, including "'oppressive pretrial incarceration,' 'anxiety and concern of the accused,' and 'the possibility that the [accused's] defense will be impaired' by dimming memories and loss of exculpatory evidence." *See Doggett v. United States*, 505 U.S. 647, 654 (1992) (citing *Barker*, 407 U.S. at 532; *Smith v. Hooey*, 393 U.S. 374, 377-379 (1969); *United States v. Ewell*, 383 U.S. 116, 120 (1966).

[93] United States v. Ghailani, 751 F. Supp. 2d 515, 534 (S.D.N.Y. 2010).

[94] *Id.* at 535. The court pointed out that the defendant had been "no more able to engage in hostilities against the United States while in the custody of the Bureau of Prisons pending trial on this indictment than he was at Guantanamo in the custody of the DoD. He could have been brought to this Court in 2006 or any subsequent date to face this 1998 indictment and, at the same time, prevented from engaging in hostilities against this country." *Id.* at 536.

[95] *Id.* at 538. The judge contrasted this factor against situations where delay is justified by ongoing state investigations and prosecutions.

[96] *Id.* at 540.

[97] United States v. Ghailani, 743 F. Supp. 2d 261 (S.D.N.Y. 2010).

search and seizure context should hold sway in the Fifth Amendment context.[98] Consequently, the court held hearings to examine whether the witness's testimony was truly voluntary; the extent to which the coerced statements played a role in securing the witness's cooperation; and whether the lapse of time between the illegal government action and contact with the witness established a sufficient attenuation to avoid the exclusion of his testimony. The judge ultimately found each of these criteria weighed in favor of the defendant, but the facts leading to this determination remain largely classified.[99]

After a jury trial, Ghailani was found guilty of conspiracy to destroy buildings and property of the United States, but not guilty of 284 other counts—one count of murder or attempted murder for each of the Americans killed or injured in the attacks, one count each for the bombing the U.S. embassies in Dar es Salaam, Tanzania, and Nairobi, Kenya, and various other charges related to the bombings.[100] The jury concluded that Ghailani's participation in the property destruction conspiracy was a direct or proximate cause of the death of a person other than a conspirator. After rejecting the defendant's motion for acquittal or a new trial on the property conspiracy charge,[101] which the defense argued was necessary in light of the seemingly inconsistent verdict,[102] the judge sentenced Ghailani to life imprisonment based on the aggravating factor the jury found.

The results of Ghailani's trial have fueled the debate over whether military commissions or federal court trials are appropriate in terrorism cases. Some observers view the trial as a demonstration that federal trial courts using the ordinary tools of criminal justice are up to the task of meting out justice to terrorists, while others characterize the outcome as a "near acquittal" that demonstrates the superiority of military commissions. The judge's post-trial opinion denying the defendant's motion for acquittal sheds some light on what may seem to be a curious verdict. Ghailani's defense throughout the trial was that he had been unknowingly duped into carrying out what he thought were innocent acts, but which in hindsight turned out to be acts in furtherance of the bombing conspiracy. The charge of conspiracy to destroy property, however, did not require that the government prove beyond a reasonable doubt that Ghailani was aware of the exact

---

[98] United States v. Ghailani, 743 F. Supp. 2d 242 (S.D.N.Y. 2010) (order). Under the "core application" doctrine, the exclusionary rule should be limited to cases where it serves as a deterrent to unlawful police actions, which typically means barring the use of unlawfully seized evidence in the government's case in chief for the offense that precipitated the search, and that extension of the rule to cases where the remedial purpose is not served (such as cases in which a search is defective due to clerical error) must be justified by weighing the additional marginal deterrence against the cost to the public interest in pursuing the truth. *See* Arizona v. Evans, 514 U.S. 1 (1995). The government argued that the exclusion of any evidence obtained as a result of Ghailani's coerced statements would not serve any deterrent purpose because the interrogation was conducted as part of a CIA effort to gather intelligence necessary for national security purposes rather than part of a law enforcement operation., and that CIA interrogators did not contemplate nor were motivated by the prospect of a criminal investigation. Judge Kaplan rejected the government's rationale, noting that a Fourth Amendment violation occurs at the time of an unlawful search or seizure, while the Fifth Amendment's Self-Incrimination Clause is violated whenever a coerced statement or its fruit is introduced at trial. Accordingly, he reasoned that the direct protection of a constitutional right rather than the deterrence of future violations was at stake in the case before him, and that the rationale of the core application doctrine did not apply.

[99] United States v. Ghailani, 743 F. Supp. 2d 261 (S.D.N.Y. 2010).

[100] For a complete list of charges, see Press Release, U.S. Justice Department, "Ahmed Ghailani Transferred from Guantanamo Bay to New York for Prosecution on Terror Charges," June 9, 2009, available at http://www.justice.gov/opa/pr/2009/June/09-ag-563.html.

[101] United States v. Ghailani, 761 F. Supp. 2d 167 (S.D.N.Y. 2011).

[102] The defense argued in essence that a conviction for conspiracy to commit a substantive offense is improper where a defendant is acquitted of committing the substantive offense itself and the proof necessary to support the substantive charge is identical to that required for a conspiracy conviction. The judge rejected that theory as a valid statement of the law. *See id.* at 190-191.

objective and targets of the plot; it merely required proof that Ghailani understood that his activities would very likely result in the bombing of American facilities somewhere, for which the judge agreed there was abundant evidence. The jury was instructed that willful blindness on the part of the accused to the precise objective of the conspiracy would invalidate a defense based on the lack of requisite knowledge, and that conviction was therefore proper if the facts demonstrated that the defendant "was aware of a high probability of the fact in dispute and consciously avoided confirming that fact"[103] In contrast, the charge for participating in the Dar es Salaam embassy bombing required proof that "Ghailani knew that the embassy was a target and that he acted to further that goal."[104] Apparently the jury did not agree that the government's evidence adequately established these elements.

Conclusion

Although the political branches of government have been primarily responsible for shaping U.S. wartime detention policy in the conflict with Al Qaeda and the Taliban, the judiciary has also played a significant role in clarifying elements of the rights and privileges owed to detainees under the Constitution and existing federal statutes and treaties. These rulings may have long-term consequences for U.S. detention policy, both in the conflict with Al Qaeda and the Taliban and in future armed conflicts. Judicial decisions concerning the meaning and effect of existing statutes and treaties may compel the executive branch to modify its current practices to conform with judicial opinion. For example, judicial opinions concerning the scope of detention authority conferred by the AUMF may inform executive decisions as to whether grounds exist to detain an individual suspected of involvement with Al Qaeda or the Taliban. Judicial decisions concerning statutes applicable to criminal prosecutions in Article III courts or military tribunals may influence executive determinations as to the appropriate forum in which to try detainees for criminal offenses.

Judicial rulings may also invite response from the legislative branch, including consideration of legislative proposals to modify existing authorities governing U.S. detention policy. The 2012 NDAA, for example, contains provisions which arguably codify aspects of existing jurisprudence regarding U.S. authority to detain persons in the conflict with Al Qaeda. Judicial activity with respect to the present armed conflict may also influence legislative activity in future hostilities. For example, Congress may look to judicial rulings interpreting the meaning and scope of the 2001 AUMF for guidance when drafting legislation authorizing the executive to use military force in some future conflict.

While the Supreme Court has issued definitive rulings concerning certain issues related to wartime detainees, many other issues related to the capture, treatment, and trial of suspected enemy belligerents are either the subject of ongoing litigation or are likely to be addressed by the judiciary. Accordingly, the courts appear likely to play a significant role in shaping U.S. policies relating to enemy belligerents in the foreseeable future.

---

[103] *Id.* at 194.
[104] *Id.*

Author Contact Information

Jennifer K. Elsea
Legislative Attorney
jelsea@crs.loc.gov, 7-5466

Michael John Garcia
Legislative Attorney
mgarcia@crs.loc.gov, 7-3873

www.ingramcontent.com/pod-product-compliance
Lightning Source LLC
Chambersburg PA
CBHW081359170526
45166CB00010B/3148